East Hill Baptist
25650 124th Ave. SE
Kent, WA. 98030
253-630-9525

A MORE SURE
WORD
WHICH BIBLE CAN YOU TRUST?

R.B. OUELLETTE

First published in 2008 by Striving Together Publications, a ministry of Lancaster Baptist Church, Lancaster, CA 93535. Striving Together Publications is committed to providing tried, trusted, and proven books that will further equip local churches to carry out the Great Commission. Your comments and suggestions are valued.

Striving Together Publications
4020 E. Lancaster Blvd.
Lancaster, CA 93535
800.201.7748

Compiled and Edited by Mike Lester
Edited by Cary Schmidt
Cover design by Jeremy Lofgren

ISBN 978-1-59894-047-3

Printed in the United States of America

TABLE OF CONTENTS

ACKNOWLEDGEMENTS

This book is a highly corroborative effort. Brother Mike Lester, academic dean of West Coast Baptist College, took the notes and recordings of my material and did yeoman's work in expanding the original information, adding helpful insights and providing valuable historical perspective. Brother Cary Schmidt, associate pastor at Lancaster Baptist Church, made further important additions and clarifications. He also created charts and chapter summaries. Dr. Paul Chappell, pastor of Lancaster Baptist Church and president of West Coast Baptist College, not only offered to do the project initially, but also invested significant time in reviewing, commenting and making valuable suggestions.

Special thanks should go to Dr. Rick Flanders, Dr. David Sorenson and Dr. Thomas Strouse, whose wise advice and constructive criticisms have been a huge help. Dr. Marty Marriott also took time to review the material and made valuable contributions.

Thanks to the loyal, faithful people of the First Baptist Church of Bridgeport for whom I initially prepared these lessons and whose helpful support has been a blessing and encouragement for over three decades. Finally, I want to thank my lovely wife and helpmate of almost thirty-five years for her encouragement and support in this project and so many other areas of my life and ministry. I love you.

*I call to God to record against the day we
shall appear before our Lord Jesus, to give
a reckoning of our doings, that I never
altered one syllable of God's Word against
my conscience, nor would I so alter it this day,
if all that is in the earth, whether it be pleasure,
honour, or riches, might be given me.*

—William Tyndale

FOREWORD

As a college student, an assistant pastor, and a young pastor, I was largely indifferent to the controversy swirling about me regarding the Bible translation issue. My attitude was, "I use the King James, I always plan to use the King James, I don't have time to get involved in all these arguments." I agreed with the man who said, "It is foolish for us to stand around fighting about our swords. We should just be using them." I sympathized with Spurgeon, who said that defending the Bible is like defending a lion in a cage. You don't need to defend it; you simply need to open the cage and let it loose. Of course, I do believe the Bible is the Sword of the Spirit and that it is quick and powerful. I frequently quote the Word of God to those who do not believe it, recognizing that their belief in it has no bearing on its effect on them.

However, as time went on, I found the issue was unavoidable. Our young people would go off to a Christian college and have their faith in the Word of God challenged. In some cases, it was weakened by classmates and professors. Our church members began to have questions brought about by discussions with co-workers, family members from other churches, or brothers in Christ who did not attend our church. So—with some reluctance and trepidation—I began my study.

I was amazed at what I learned. I had no idea how many verses in the new translations weakened vital doctrines of the Word of God. I found it astounding that men with such unorthodox doctrinal positions had been leaders in promoting and preparing a new Greek text. On the other hand, I found myself thrilled to see how wonderfully and carefully God has preserved His Word for His people.

In John 17:8, our Lord prays these words, "*For I have given unto them the words which thou gavest me; and they have received them....*" Jude states that we are to contend for the faith that has been once delivered to the saints. There are essentially two positions in Bible-believing circles regarding the Word of God. The first one states, "We have it...." The second one believes, "We have it in a body of manuscripts and we're still working on getting it into English." In other words, "We have most of it, and we are working on the rest." Now, those who take this position generally would not state it this way, but this is the logical conclusion of the position—a position that leads to constant ongoing revision work. In other words, some believe in a *preserved* Word and others believe in a *progressive* Word. Some believe in truth that has been *delivered* and others believe in truth that is still being *discovered*—at least as far as the English language is concerned. If the Bible is true—and it is—then God's Word is preserved for us and we possess it. (If the Bible is not true, we have no foundation for our faith, and are subject to the winds of change, the whims of society, and the opinions of man.) Thank God for His preserved Word!

I also want to note that in a study of this subject, it is inevitable that names of individuals will be used to represent the differing positions with the issue of Bible preservation. The use of the names in this book is neither a personal attack nor an endorsement of those men.

I am often asked why men like Dr. John R. Rice and Dr. Noel Smith took a different position on the Bible issue than I and so many others do today. Of course, the only honest answer is, I don't know—they're not available for me to ask. I have tremendous respect for both of these men—they were giants who had a huge influence on our country and our world. It is fair to say that this issue is relatively new, and the majority of the debate began near the end of their ministries. A large amount of information has been published and much truth has been made available since these men have gone on to Heaven.

I believe that good and sincere Christians use other translations of the Bible. This book is not intended to impugn them or their integrity in any way. As a Christian brother, I respect their work for the Lord and their liberty to choose the text that they believe to be the Word of God. While the Word of God has many enemies in this world today, Bible-believing Christians on both sides of this issue are not the enemy to God's Word nor to each other. May you read this book with the respect that is intended to believers on both sides of the issue.

Dr. R.B. Ouellette
First Baptist Church
Bridgeport, MI

PREFACE

The book you are holding in your hand is written by a man whose soundness in doctrine and personal integrity has been an encouragement to me and to pastors all across America.

Perhaps you have heard this statement: "I have always considered the actions of a man to be the best interpreter of his thoughts." The actions of Dr. R.B. Ouellette have been those of a man who consistently teaches and preaches and lives out the Word of God. His passion for God is strong and his spirit in ministry is kind.

Unfortunately, this characteristic is not commonly found with men who have written books and articles pertaining to the preservation of the Scriptures. For years I have heard men declare their confidence in the King James Bible without giving a reasonable explanation for that confidence.

It has been my personal experience that many men who write about the Bible rarely witness and lead others to the Lord Jesus

Christ. What you are about to read does not come merely from a man with a strong understanding of the doctrine of preservation, but from a man who consistently shares the preserved truths of the Gospel. On many occasions I have personally been with Dr. Ouellette when he has shared the Gospel and led someone to Jesus Christ.

This book is not written as a mere academic pursuit or by one looking for another theological argument. It is written by a man who is passionate about the message of the Cross and the veracity of the Scriptures.

I am delighted that Striving Together Publications could partner with Dr. Ouellette in this effort, as I believe there is a need for this work amongst Bible-believing Christians. Our heart in this manuscript is not to be caustic, sarcastic, or to unfairly represent those who hold different view points. It is simply to communicate— with a right spirit—the facts and truths that we believe to be so essential to the subject.

As you open the following pages and consider the subject of the preservation of the Scriptures, it is our prayer that you will stand with confidence and in the power of the Holy Spirit to share the wonderful message of the Gospel with this lost and dying world.

It is my prayer that you will be greatly encouraged and strengthened by what you are about to read!

Paul Chappell, Pastor and President
Lancaster Baptist Church
West Coast Baptist College

Introduction

The U.S. Federal Aviation Administration has a unique way of testing the strength of airplane windshields. Engineers created a gun that launches a dead chicken into the windshield at the approximate speed that the airplane would be flying. The theory is, if the window doesn't crack or break, it could survive the impact of a bird in flight.

British aerospace engineers heard about this unique device and wanted to use it to run the same sort of tests on a high-speed locomotive they were developing. So, they borrowed the FAA's "chicken launcher," skimmed the instructions, loaded it and fired. To their surprise, the ballistic chicken immediately shattered the windshield, went through the engineer's chair, and smashed the instrument panel.

The British engineers were stunned and immediately contacted the FAA. After reviewing the procedures of the British engineers to determine if the test was done properly, the FAA had only one recommendation, "Thaw the chicken."

A lot of damage can be done by missing one detail in the instructions!

With this in mind, as you begin this book, I would like to ask a favor—please don't "skim" the contents. Would you determine to read the entire book (including the foreword and preface if you skipped them)? There is much to be said in this study, and much can be misunderstood or taken out of context. I strongly believe that to understand the whole heart and message of this book, you must read it in its entirety. Questions that arise early in the book may be addressed in more detail later, so please read on.

Then, please know from the start that I have made every effort to be precise and accurate with the facts about this issue without getting "bogged down" by them and distracted from the heart of the issue. We will cover many historical details and facts related to Bible versions and their translations. If, as a reader, you find that I have misstated anything, please understand that this is not because of any deliberate effort to manipulate the information in favor of my argument. As we study this topic, it is my sincere desire to represent both sides of the issue truthfully and respectfully, while at the same time stating why I believe in the King James Bible.

When I was a boy, there was no controversy regarding the Bible. The Revised Standard Version, which was published in 1952, had been soundly rejected by virtually all orthodox, Bible-believing

---

DEFINING THE TERMS

Translation: *The efforts of men, hopefully but not always under God's guidance, to render God's Word into another language.*

Inspiration: *The recording, or giving of God's Word; "God-breathed." (See expanded definition, p. 185.)*

Christians as weakening basic doctrinal truths. The American Standard Version, though used by R.A. Torrey, was the preferred Bible of only a small segment of evangelical Christianity. Nearly everyone in fundamental or evangelical Christianity used the King James Version. Some possessed other **translations** which they used essentially as one would use a commentary. However, the Bible that was preached from, read publicly, used for devotions, and employed in evangelism was almost universally the King James Version.

I was a young college student when I first heard a graduate student preach from the New American Standard Bible. He carefully said, "This is one of only two translations that I would recommend to you." In my youth and inexperience, I accepted his statement. Not long after that, I spoke to an older and wiser preacher about the New American Standard Bible. He said, "Well, there's a problem with that version. In 2 Timothy 3:16 the footnote raises questions as to *which part* of Scripture is inspired. It reads 'every scripture inspired by God is also profitable.'"

That was enough for me to have no further interest in the NASB. What a small and yet exceedingly significant question to raise. The Bible with which I had grown up declared affirmatively, unequivocally and boldly that all Scripture is inspired of God. This new Bible simply implied that perhaps only those portions of the scripture which were inspired were profitable. (While it is true that this error is based on a mis-translation in the 1901 ASV and is not based on a textual issue, it nonetheless demonstrates the mind-set of those who edited and translated this version.) Of course, the immediate series of questions that came to mind was, "Which portions of scripture did these translators think were not inspired? How was one to know what scripture is inspired and what is not? What else is in the Bible that shouldn't be there?"

The issue of **inspiration** began to percolate in my mind when I left home at the age of fifteen to attend my last year of high school in a school operated by a well-known Christian college. I was reviewing the teaching from my Bible class and said to my college roommates, "I want to get this straight. So God inspired every word of the Bible." My roommates immediately informed me that this was inaccurate. My position as I had articulated it, they told me, was "mechanical dictation."

"Oh," I said, "Then God inspired the thoughts rather than the words."

"No!" they responded with alarm. "That's Liberalism."

I remember as a fifteen or sixteen-year-old thinking to myself, "I wonder what's more than the thoughts and less than the words?" I have yet to find an answer to that question!

Later on, when I attended college, I remember a teacher telling us that certain portions of scripture were probably added by "an over-zealous scribe." My thoughts began to race in this fashion once again: "You mean there are things in the Bible that don't belong there? What else is in the Bible that shouldn't exist? How do you know? Who was this scribe? When did he live? What else did he mess up?"

For many years, I did not make a major issue of the Bible translation controversy. I simply encouraged our church family to use the King James Version.

One reason for this is that some who promoted the KJV were characterized by intemperate speech, unkind behavior, and an un-Christ-like spirit. While I found myself in basic agreement with their position, their disposition did nothing to attract me to them. Others took such extreme stands as alleging that only those led to Christ through the use of the King James Bible were actually saved. They said that if someone had sincerely trusted Christ as their Saviour but had been given the Gospel from the New International Version, they were born again, not as a child of God, but as a child of the devil!

In recent years, new books on this subject, which are critical of the KJV, have been directed specifically towards laymen and individual church members. As a Pastor and an undershepherd, this has alarmed me. For some time the battle over Bible versions had largely been among preachers. The publishers of these recent books have now directed their information to lay people. Many things from these books have concerned me, one of which is a statement by John E. Ashbrook, who said that the King James was the "Model T" of Bible translations. He continued his analogy by saying that the Model T was a great improvement in transportation—a breakthrough, a tremendous innovation. However, he said, it would have been "a tragedy" if the automobile industry had stopped with the Model T.[1] (By the way, this particular statement says more than the author intended and indicates one of the problems of those who argue for "new" translations. For many of them, the Bible is always a work in progress and never a completed project. There are always more manuscripts to be found, more changes to be made, more improvements to be accomplished.) If this analogy is correct, it is a tragedy every time I preach from my King James Bible—a tragedy every time I have my devotions from the KJV—a tragedy every time I witness to someone using my Authorized Version.

As I began my study of the translation issue, I presented it to the members of our church over a period of several months on Wednesday nights. By faith, I was persuaded that I was using the right Bible, but I must confess, I had some reservations about what the facts would reveal. I wondered what I might find as I waded into this complicated subject and read "the experts." I suppose I read thirty to forty books and major articles on this issue in that study. I was careful to read books from both sides, including James White's *The King James Only Controversy* and D. A. Carson's *The King James Version Debate: A Plea for Realism*. I was amazed at what I learned. This is a complicated issue and either side has difficult questions. However, the facts—the weight of the evidence—are clearly on the side of our old KJV Bible. There are always those who will ask, "What difference does it make? Does it really matter? Aren't the changes so small and insignificant that they are irrelevant? Haven't we been told repeatedly that no 'major doctrine' is affected by the differences in translations? Isn't it, as one former pastor was fond of saying, 'ridiculous for us to be defending our Sword'?"

In brief: Yes, it does matter. Many of the changes are indeed significant. Many more examples will be given in this material, but two brief ones suffice:

First, **B.F. Westcott and J.A. Hort**, the promulgators and promoters of the new Greek **text** which has strongly influenced all modern Bible translations, alleged (with others before them) that the last twelve verses of the book of Mark do not belong there. How did twelve extra, uninspired verses get into the KJV Bible? Would not this cause an individual to question what other passages may have been added? (The scholars' term for this is "**conflation**" or a "conflated reading.") Second, in John 7, the KJV Bible quotes the Lord Jesus as saying, *"I go not up yet unto this feast."* However, the New International Version has our Saviour saying, "I go not up to the feast." Since He does go, the KJV Bible accurately depicts Him as delaying His departure where the new Bible depicts Him as dishonestly saying He is *not* going to do what He then *does.*

A family who came from a non–King James church once visited our church. When I went to see them, they brought up the Bible issue. I had them open their parallel translation of the NIV and the KJV and showed them this passage in John seven. The lady became quite agitated and said, "Why, I'm going to cross that out!"

NOTABLE NAMES

Brooke F. Westcott and Fenton John Anthony Hort: *Two men who published a new Greek text in 1881. The English Revised Version of the Bible was the first translation from that text in 1881. Their work in textual criticism laid the foundation for most future new Bible translations. (See expanded definition, p. 195.)*

I appreciated her willingness to make a correction. But I wondered why she would wish to keep and use a translation in which she would have to make individual corrections.

If I wanted to corrupt the Word of God, I would not do so dramatically, but by small degrees. No one would believe a Bible translation to be correct which said, "Jesus is a mere man" or "the Lord Jesus did not rise bodily from the grave." Such blasphemy would be treated as a fraud.

However, several changes over a period of time can unalterably erode precious Bible doctrines. The Scriptures warn us to *"Remove not the ancient landmark, which thy fathers have set"* (Proverbs 22:28). I am told that property boundaries were often marked by a row of stones. A person wishing to steal property from his neighbor would simply move his stones. Now, to move them a large distance would be obvious, so the clever neighbor would just move them a foot or two at a time. A difference so small and imperceptible as to go unnoticed, yet by their gradual removal, precious land would be lost. So, too, I fear, the gradual diminishing of the truth of Scripture could cause many to never fully understand and embrace the faith *"once delivered unto the saints."*

DEFINING THE TERMS

Text: A compilation of manuscript evidence that is used to form the Bible. There are three competing texts for translational purposes: 1) Received Text, 2) Critical Text, and 3) Majority Text (though some classify this as synonymous with the Received Text.) (See expanded definition, p. 190.)

Conflation: An attempt to fuse together; merger of two or more things or ideas into one. In textual criticism, it is the belief of some scholars that the Byzantine Text is a merger of Alexandrian and Western texts. This allows for Byzantine readings before AD 400. This is also called the Lucian Recension or the Syrian Recension theory.

The position of this book is simple: The King James Bible is the right translation for English-speaking Christians to use because it is a literal translation of the correct and pure Greek and Hebrew texts. Those who believe that the critical Greek texts are more accurate and more reliable than the **Received Text** (from which our King James Bible is translated, sometimes referred to as the TR, Textus Receptus, or Traditional Text) must answer the question, "Why did God keep His Word from His people for over 1,800 years?" The answer? He did not.

I must plead guilty to circular reasoning. My position on the Bible did not start with **manuscript** evidence, study of books written on the translation issue, or other scholarly offerings. It started with the Word of God. In a host of Scriptures, many of which will be quoted later in this publication, God promises to preserve His Word. If we accept the Scripture as being true, we must accept the TR (the Received Text) position over the new Greek texts of recent centuries. This proven Greek text is the only one that is consistent with the preservation promises of the Word of God.

> I heard the old-time preacher speak
> Without one reference to the Greek,
> "This precious Book within my hand
> Is God's own Word on which I stand."

DEFINING THE TERMS

Received Text (Traditional Text): This phrase is used to refer to the biblical manuscripts that authentic churches and Christians have accepted since the inception of the local church. (See expanded definition, p. 189.)

Manuscripts: Hand-written, ancient copies of Scriptures from a multiplicity of cultures, languages, and eras.

And then the scholars came along
    And said the preacher had it wrong:
"Conflations here, recensions there,
    And scribal errors everywhere.

A book 'essentially correct,'
    But not in every last respect."
"A 'fairly certain' Word," they say,
    "To light our path and guide our way."

Then in despair I bowed my head.
    "We have no Word of God," I said.
"If some of this old Book is wrong,
    Pray tell, what else does not belong?"

Will still more manuscripts be found
    To make us go another round?
Correcting, changing, taking out;
    Creating questions, fear and doubt?

Must more discoveries come to light
    Before we finally get it right?
Will precious doctrines fade away
    Because of what the scholars say?

How many "errors" must we purge
    Because of what the scholars urge?
How many versions must we make?
    How many changes can we take?

How will we ever know we're through—
    That we possess a Scripture true?
If man must find God's Word, my friend,
    When will the changes ever end?

Then to the Book again I fled
To find out what my Father said.
"Forever settled…never fade"—
This promise God the Spirit made.

A thousand generations hence—
That seems a pretty strong defense.
A "perfect Book"? Then it must be
Man can't improve what God gave me.

We have a Book completely true,
Instructing us in all we do.
Preserved by God, not found by men,
Inscribed by God the Spirit's pen.

If God or scholars you must choose,
Be sure the "experts" always lose.
Don't give to them a second look;
Just keep believing this old Book.

Written by R.B. Ouellette

CHAPTER ONE IN SUMMARY

1. The current translation debate is a relatively new debate amongst Bible-believing Christians.

2. The translation debate wrestles with significant doctrinal differences, not just minor changes between Bibles.

3. The two sides of the debate generally have two different views of "preservation."

4. New Bible versions are based upon a new Greek text put forth by Westcott and Hort in the late 1800s.

5. Many modern Bible scholars believe in a "conflation theory" that early Christians and scribes intentionally added to the Word of God.

6. The King James Bible was based upon the Received Text which we believe to be the only reliable text.

Understanding the Spirit of the Discussion

For we have not followed cunningly devised fables, when we made known unto you the power and coming of our Lord Jesus Christ, but were eyewitnesses of his majesty. For he received from God the Father honour and glory, when there came such a voice to him from the excellent glory, This is my beloved Son, in whom I am well pleased. And this voice which came from heaven we heard, when we were with him in the holy mount. We have also a more sure word of prophecy; whereunto ye do well that ye take heed, as unto a light that shineth in a dark place, until the day dawn, and the day star arise in your hearts: Knowing this first, that no prophecy of the scripture is of any private interpretation. For the prophecy came not in old time by the will of man: but holy men of God spake as they were moved by the Holy Ghost."—2 PETER 1:16–21

> *"All scripture is given by inspiration of God, and is profitable for doctrine, for reproof, for correction, for instruction in righteousness: That the man of God may be perfect, throughly furnished unto all good works."*
> —2 Timothy 3:16–17

The title of this book, *A More Sure Word*, comes from 2 Peter 1:19. As we notice this verse in its context, we understand that Peter is referring to the incident that took place on the Mount of Transfiguration, a truly life-changing moment. He was one of only three who were privileged to see Moses and Elijah talking with Jesus.

Peter begins to argue that they have not followed "cunningly devised fables." This was not a message he received second hand. He was there personally on the Mount. In this passage, Peter reminds his audience that he was an eyewitness of His majesty when Christ received glory and honor. He goes on to say that he was an ear-witness to the voice of God coming from Heaven.

Peter saw the glorified Christ and heard the voice of God from Heaven. He saw and heard something that made an impact on his life. Few people would have the same privilege as Peter, and with this privilege he emphatically states that "we have also a more sure word of prophecy." What is this "more sure word" that is to be trusted over what eyes have seen or ears have heard? It is the powerful, preserved Word of God.

In this same passage, we read that *"no prophecy of the scripture is of any private interpretation."* This verse has been often misconstrued. It does not mean that we must go to a priest, a scholar, or an expert to get the meaning of a verse because we cannot understand it "privately." Consider the fact that the Author and Interpreter of Scripture has permanently indwelt every believer and promises to guide them into all truth (John 16:13). This statement actually means that no Scripture stands by itself. It must be interpreted in the light of other Scriptures. Passages that seem obscure must be seen in light of more clear passages. For further proof that the "scholar" is not the only one who can give a correct interpretation of Scripture, consider who is writing the epistle—an unlearned, ignorant fisherman.

This passage teaches much about the way God worked to give us His Word. We find the Initiator is the Holy Ghost. These words are the words of God. They are called "God-breathed" (literal meaning of "given by inspiration of God") in 2 Timothy 3:16. In Matthew 4:4, Jesus states that man is to live by every word that proceeds from God. Paul understood that his letters were to be received as the Word of God in 1 Thessalonians 2:13. It is the "Word of God" that is quick and powerful. Peter declares boldly that these words have come directly from the Holy Ghost.

The instruments used to pen these words were holy men. While God can do the impossible, He has chosen to send His God-breathed Word to us through the agency of holy men. It is still a biblical mandate for us to be holy as He is holy (1 Peter 1:16). When the Holy Spirit prepared to give this world the Word of God, He did so through the instrumentality of holy men.

When the Holy Ghost gave His Word through holy men, the truths they recorded were described as "holy scriptures." In 2 Timothy 3:15, Paul reminded Timothy that it was the holy Scriptures he knew from his childhood that were able to produce salvation within him. This reference makes it clear that God intends the Bible to be our trustworthy final authority in all matters of faith and practice.

According to 2 Timothy 3:16, *"All scripture is given by inspiration of God"* (God-breathed). Yet, here is a glimpse of just one of the major translational differences that have led to the very reason for this book. Compare this verse in the King James with the American Standard Version which was published in 1901:

2 Timothy 3:16—KJV
*"**All scripture is given by inspiration** of God, and is profitable for doctrine, for reproof, for correction, for instruction in righteousness."*

2 Timothy 3:16—ASV

"**Every scripture inspired** of God is also profitable for teaching, for reproof, for correction, for instruction which is in righteousness."

If someone reads, "Every scripture inspired of God is also profitable," questions are raised in his mind. How does he know *which* scripture is inspired of God and which is not? If only the *inspired* verses are profitable, does that mean that the *uninspired* verses in his Bible are not profitable? With only a small change in this one verse, man has now become the final judge of which scripture is profitable. With this small change, the Bible moves from being "totally inspired," that is "*All scripture is given by inspiration of God,*" to being only "partially inspired." That's a major change!

(The fact that the ASV has long since been rejected by Bible-believing Christians only strengthens the argument that modern-day textual criticism believes the English Bible to be an ongoing work in progress which can always be improved upon.)

If you only have a partially-inspired Bible, how do you know which part is *inspired*? If you have a partially preserved Bible, how do you know which part is *preserved*? And why wouldn't God preserve all of His intended Word for us? There are those who believe the scholars are to make these decisions for us. According to George Eldon Ladd in his book on **textual criticism**, "It also means that in the search for a good text, piety and devotion can never take the place of knowledge and scholarly judgment. One does not solve

---

DEFINING THE TERMS

Textual Criticism: Refers to the study of manuscripts or printings to determine the original or most authoritative form of a text. Whether one holds to a Received Text or a Critical Text, textual criticism has been employed with both of these texts. There are two types of textual criticism which determine how a textual critic approaches the Bible— one based upon belief and one based upon unbelief.

---

a problem of divergent textual readings by prayer or by inner illumination of the Holy Spirit, but only by an extensive knowledge and skill in the science of textual criticism."[1]

According to Ladd, God in His providence has committed these matters for the scholars to decide. This is quite contrary to the practice of the true church (local assemblies of baptized believers) over the centuries where personal study and public readings were of central importance to searching out the Scriptures. (Acts 17:11, "...they received the word with all readiness of mind, and searched the scriptures daily, whether those things were so.") This is where our belief in the "priesthood of every believer" should be a reality.

During the days that gave birth to the Reformation, there lived a man named Thomas Hawkes. Most Christians will live their entire lives without ever hearing his name. Yet, his story illustrates this principle of an institution attempting to keep the common man from God's Word.

Hawkes had served as a page in the courts of Edward VI of England. He had embraced the Reformers' faith. When Edward died, religion changed and those of the Reformers' persuasion were in danger.

Rather than change his faith, Hawkes took his family back to the area of Esses. Here, his wife gave birth to a son. Hawkes refused to have his child baptized by the Romish priests and so hid his child for three weeks.

His enemies had him charged with being unsound in religion. Particularly, three charges were leveled against him: 1) He refused to have his child christened. 2) He refused to hear the Mass in Latin. 3) He read and studied the Bible for himself.

On February 8, 1555, Edmund Bonner, Bishop of London, condemned Hawkes as a heretic for these "serious crimes." He was sentenced to die with Thomas Watts on June 10, 1555.

His friends were apprehensive. They knew it would not be long before they too were found out and forced to embrace the stake and the fire. They asked for a sign from Hawkes. If his mind was still at peace in the flames, would he simply raise his hands toward Heaven?

On that fateful day, the fire quickly took the voice away from Hawkes. When in the fire so long that he could no longer speak—his skin had shrunk, his fingers had burned off, and everyone thought he was dead—he suddenly raised his burning hands over his head and clapped them together three times. The people, especially those who understood the significance, broke into praise and applause as Thomas Hawkes slipped into eternity.

This story could be duplicated many times over. This desire to remove the Bible from the common people did not originate with God. It was the common people who heard Him gladly. The New Testament was written in what has been called "Koine" Greek—the language of the common people. It is, of course, our conviction that every individual needs the Word of God.

This is no longer a question for preachers solely to struggle with this in their study. The battle ground is now in the pews of our local churches. Many present-day authors are not kind in their reference to the King James Bible, and do not believe that it is the authoritative Word of God for English-speaking people. They are often more sympathetic towards the **Critical Text** (also called the Eclectic Text).

As we begin, I would like to share the heart and intent of this book. So many on both sides of this issue have a caustic and harsh

---

DEFINING THE TERMS

Critical Text: *This "new" Greek text put forth in the late 1800s, is an attempt to reconstruct or restore the true Bible text of the New Testament by assigning a higher importance to the few "oldest manuscripts" rather than trusting the larger body of evidence in the Received Text. (See expanded definition, p. 187.)*

---

spirit, and that is not the intention of these pages. Allow me to share with you ten introductory statements that will help open the door for this subject in the coming chapters:

1. This is a serious issue which affects fundamental doctrine. It is of utmost importance that we know whether "all scripture is inspired" or "every scripture that is inspired...." We need to know whether it is "God [who] was manifest in the flesh" or "He who was manifest in the flesh...." (Both the New American Standard and New International Version have "he" rather than "God.") Both you and I are "manifest in the flesh." What does that mean? It certainly does not mean that we are God. Yet 1 Timothy 3:16—which is a strong verse on the deity of Christ—has been watered down and weakened with the change of one word: "God" to "he."

In other words, the translation issue is not merely about updating archaic words or "King James" English, as some believe. The new translations contain doctrinal differences that should matter to every Christian.

2. Taking a different position does not necessarily make a man a heretic. While I may be labeled a heretic for making that statement, we must see the real issue at stake. This issue is not always a "good" versus "bad." For the most part, this issue among true Christians is about good people disagreeing with other good people. I have good friends who do not take the same position I do on the preservation of Scripture. This does not make them heretics. They are orthodox in their doctrine and they believe the fundamentals of the faith. They believe in the inspiration of Scriptures.

There are many different positions on this issue. One educator has identified ten different positions where people draw the lines on this issue. Taking a different position does not mean a person is a heretic and does not mean they should be treated as an enemy.

3. There are good people and non-discerning speech on both sides of the debate. There are men on both sides of this debate who have used harsh and critical speech and who have taken extreme and unwise positions. It is wrong to automatically label someone who believes in the veracity of the King James Bible as "extreme or harsh" simply because of these types of men. In like manner, it would be wrong to label a proponent of the Critical Text as a fan of "Westcott and Hort" simply because they believe the Critical Text to be a better Greek text. Using a broad brush in this manner is unfair to reasonable and right-spirited people on both sides of the discussion. We should remember that the devil is the enemy—not a Christian brother who uses a different Bible version!

4. Both sides of this discussion have difficult questions. This book will not answer all the questions that are raised against the position I take. However, *I am happier with the questions I cannot answer than the questions that the other side cannot answer.* I once read this statement by D.L. Moody that I find applicable here: "When I find things in the Bible that are above my reasoning, I am reminded that it is God's Word and not mine."

5. Both sides have been characterized by intemperate speech. There are many who use the King James Bible who have been characterized by intemperate speech, yet at the same time, one Baptist seminary calls those who take the King James only position as "cultic and heterodox..."[2]—nice words. By their definition, if I am "King James only," I am described by words that could be considered intemperate and offensive. This kind of infighting only weakens the impact of the Gospel on lost people everywhere. Nothing is gained and much is lost where this kind of spirit prevails among Christians.

6. Very few people have studied the issue carefully. As I interview preachers in an attempt to learn as much as possible, I find that not many have really studied a great deal on this subject. During my study, I met only one pastor who had actually read more on the subject than I had read. I am a student, not a scholar.

Yet, what I find is that most pastors have not researched this subject. Many simply take the position that they were handed by their colleges or mentors.

This subject is worth studying carefully, if for no other reason than that you make an informed decision—especially as you consider your influence as a Christian.

7. In general, those who support the Textus Receptus (which the KJV is based upon) have been more willing than their opponents to consider and answer the arguments of the other side. In a debate, one typically gives the position of the opponent and then shows why that particular argument is wrong. This is not what I find in the "anti-KJV" literature.

For example, consider this quote by Gordon Fee: "For over 1,400 years the NT was copied by hand, and the copyists [scribes] made every conceivable error, as well as at times intentionally altering [probably with the idea of "correcting"] the text. Such errors and alterations survived in various ways, with the basic tendency to accumulate [scribes seldom left anything out, lest they omit something inspired]."[3]

"Every conceivable error" is a very broad assertion that should be supported in some way. However, no examples were given. Consider the mathematical formula that would need to be used to make sure that this claim of "every conceivable error" is a "qualified" statement and not simply a broad stroke. The truth that defeats Mr. Fee's statement is that there are over 5,600 extant manuscripts that are overwhelmingly in agreement, so as to leave no serious doubt as to the true text.

When people question those of us who use the King James Bible, we have tried to give answers. We have attempted to show how careful the scribes were in copying the manuscripts. We have attempted to show facts that can be documented or qualified. Too many times, this is missing from those who prefer the use of Bibles coming from the Critical Text—even though many of these would agree that the King James is an accurate translation. There are many bold statements made with the intent of changing someone's mind, but too often those statements contain no specific examples or documentation.

8. There is a great deal of inconsistency and some dishonesty on this issue. I believe in studying and stating what the Bible says. I also believe that some people have carried that idea overboard. I have a book in my library which takes about a third of a page to instruct its readers on the proper methodology of interpreting Scripture. The writer says that it is only after we have done these things, and only then, that we can preach with authority. A book published by faculty members of a Baptist seminary states something similar: "We believe that investigating and probing the abundance of available manuscript evidence that is accessible to the serious student has merit. Then we can preach and teach with the authority of true biblicists, speaking God's absolute truth accurately, passionately, and relevantly...."[4]

If these statements were true, then men like Bob Jones, Sr., Billy Sunday, or D.L. Moody could not have preached with authority. For those who are of this view, you cannot simply read the Bible and understand it on your own. According to this philosophy, if you do not look up the word in the Greek New Testament, you cannot know what God said and you cannot share it as a true biblicist. If that is really the case, we need to tell Christians not to read their Bibles daily until they have learned and studied Greek. It should be noted that those who hold a strong conviction for the Received Text and its translation are not against studying books or studying the Greek. We simply do not believe that biblical interpretation is limited to those who have higher education and know the Greek language. While Critical Text scholars would not admit to this position, it certainly is implied. At the very least, their position implies that there is some deeper level of understanding or superior knowledge that is available exclusively to those who know the Greek and Hebrew.

Furthermore, pastors who are of the persuasion that mastery of the biblical languages is a must would not tell their members to disregard God's Word. Yet this is the logical conclusion if a distinction is to be made between the "learned" and the "laity." The Bible calls this Nicolaitanism (carrying the idea of lording over the people or the laity) and says that God hates the establishment of a hierarchy (whether priest or scholar) between Himself and the common man. (Revelation 2:6, *"But this thou hast, that thou hatest the deeds of the Nicolaitans, which I also hate."*)

Many times, this type of writer or scholar will make statements such as, "God has never promised to preserve His Word in the Bible." If that is the case, why worry about being so "precise" in our study since we don't know if we have the right Word to begin with!

Another example of inconsistencies would be to use the King James Bible while believing that the Critical Text is a better Greek text. To further this example, consider the inconsistency of a college or seminary that uses the King James in its teaching and preaching ministries, but in the Greek class uses one of the **Nestle-Aland** editions of the Critical Text. This is inconsistent and confusing at best.

9. Taking an extreme position on either side is dangerous. Some on the side of the King James go so far as to say that you can correct the Greek from the King James. Others say that you cannot be saved unless it is through the use of a King James Bible. These

---

NOTABLE NAMES

Nestle and Aland: *Two German textual editors whose Greek texts form the basis for much of the modern New Testament translations.*

---

statements are both absurd and distract from the central issues at hand.

Critical Text proponents believe that the King James Bible was translated from a conflated text used by Christendom for 1,500 years, and that this text was never correct. It took the discovery of a manuscript in the Vatican and one in a Greek monastery on Mount Sinai to find "God's Word." Again, these assertions are absurd and they avoid the important questions.

Both of these kinds of extreme positions are dangerous. If you accept the Westcott and Hort position (which we will define in the coming chapters), why did God keep His Word from people for 1,800 years? If you accept the other extreme, you must ask, "why did God keep His Word from people for 1,600 years? Was there a Word of God before 1611?" The obvious answer is "yes!"

In either of these extreme positions, God kept His "best" Word from previous generations until He was either able to orchestrate a translation authorized by King James or until He was able to guide "manuscript hunters" to the oldest and best "lost" manuscripts.

10. It is not always necessary to separate with a brother over his position on the King James Version. Sometimes, men will use the King James Bible for different reasons than those I present in this book. One man may use the King James because of traditional reasons or reasons of uniformity rather than textual reasons. Another man's textual persuasion may be Critical Text, but his translational persuasion is King James. While we disagree on a textual position, it doesn't necessarily mean we have to separate. (Obviously we could not work together on ministry projects that involve the translating and printing of the Word of God.)

It bears repeating that, while the Word of God has many enemies throughout the world today, Bible-believing Christians on both sides of this discussion are not enemies to God's Word nor to each other. May you read these pages and receive these words with the spirit in which they are intended. If you are a Christian brother and you choose a different position after reading this book, you are still my brother and together we still have a call to reach this lost world with the Gospel of Jesus Christ. May this subject not distract us from that high calling!

Received Text Synonyms
Traditional Text
Preserved Text
Byzantine Text
Majority Text (until 1982)
Antiochan Text
Syrian Text
Textus Receptus
Western Text
TR

Critical Text Synonyms
Eclectic Text
Minority Text
Egyptian Text
Alexandrian Text
Westcott and Hort Text
Nestle-Aland Text
UBS Text

5

CHAPTER TWO IN SUMMARY

1.   God did not appoint scholars to be the final authorities for the interpretation of Scripture.

2.   Many modern scholars believe that laymen are not equipped to determine the true source of God's Word.

3.   Bible-believing Christians do not believe in a "partially-inspired" Word of God.

4.   Textual Criticism is the study of Bible manuscripts to determine the authoritative text.

5.   In the first-century church, private study and public readings were of central importance to searching out the Scriptures.

6.   The Critical Text is a new Greek text of the New Testament based upon fewer but older manuscripts.

7.   Many Bible-believing Christians disagree on the Bible issue, and both sides have difficult questions.

8.   Our spirit towards others who disagree with us should remain Christ honoring.

9.   There are extreme positions on both sides of this issue, and buried under the cloak of scholarship, there is even some dishonesty.

Understanding the Terms

Throughout these pages we will introduce terms that are central to this study. At the back of the book you will find a glossary of terms and important names with extended definitions for your reference. Also, in line with the text (as you have already seen) you will find boldfaced words and their abbreviated definitions at the bottom of the page. It is important that you pause to understand these terms and know these names as they play a major role in helping you understand the facts.

There are also biblical terms that are worthy of our earnest study. These terms are the very foundation of our discussion and contain the basis for God's promise of a preserved Word. Let's look more closely at these terms.

Inspiration—God breathed His Word.

The classic passage that deals with inspiration is 2 Timothy 3:16: "*All scripture is given by inspiration of God, and is profitable for doctrine, for reproof, for correction, for instruction in righteousness.*"

We believe the *extent* of inspiration is to all Scripture. I know I may be accused of circular reasoning. I confess to having an *a priori* assumption, a pre-supposition that the Bible is the Word of God. I start with the Bible and believe it corrects science and history, and other fields of study. It is my absolute authority.

Consider these examples: Scientists used to believe that the stars could be numbered, but now we know they cannot be counted, as God indicated to Abraham in Genesis 15:5. (Although, God numbers and names every star according to Psalm 147:4.) Science used to think that the world was flat, but now believe that the Bible is correct in speaking about the circle of the earth (Isaiah 40:22).

Science used to imagine the world was resting on something, but now believe the Bible is correct when it states that God hung the world upon nothing (Job 26:7). In each of these instances, science caught up with the Bible!

Inspiration means "God-breathed." Charles Ryrie makes this observation: "The Bible originates as an action of God who breathed it out."[1]

Additionally, we believe the *effect* of inspiration is noted in the phrase *"is profitable."* These inspired words are profitable for doctrine—what is right. They are profitable for reproof—what is not right. They are profitable for correction—how to get it right. They are profitable for instruction—how to keep it right. The desired result is that the man of God becomes totally equipped, throughly furnished, to do every good work that God has called him to do.

There is a second passage used as a parallel to 2 Timothy 3:16 —2 Peter 1:21, states: *"For the prophecy came not in old time by the will of man: but holy men of God spake as they were moved by the Holy Ghost."*

Sometimes people think there is a logical contradiction. "If all the words are from God, then why does each writer have a different style?" Here is an analogy that I hope will help. When you go to a symphony, how many want to hear all trumpets? How about just the bass? Cellos alone? Only the triangle? No, the orchestra sounds best when all the instruments are harmonizing together.

Now God doesn't just use any available instrument. The Word of God was complete in Heaven before any human instrument was used ("*For ever, O Lord, thy word is settled in heaven.*" —Psalm 119:89). He made the instruments so that they would give the right sound. He gave them the background, the culture, and the experiences needed to accomplish His desire. He not only wrote the score; He also made the instruments!

Here, we find the *marvel* of inspiration; it is a more sure Word. Peter had seen Jesus and had heard the voice of God on the Mount of Transfiguration. I wish I could have been there! I wonder what Jesus looks like, how tall He is, and how His voice sounds. However, our faith is not based on an eyewitness account. He states that we have something more reliable, more sure, more certain than that. We have the Word of God.

Hence, we would describe our belief concerning the Bible as follows:

1. We believe in verbal inspiration.
   By verbal, we mean that God gave the very words to these men. For example, Deuteronomy 31:24 states: "*And it came to pass, when Moses had made an end of writing the words of this law in a book, until they were finished….*" We believe that God did not merely give thoughts, or inspiring feelings, but that He gave the words to these men.

2. We believe in plenary inspiration.
   By plenary, we mean that the Scriptures are "fully complete" or "inspired equally." We believe that the Bible is fully the Word of God—His thoughts fully expressed. Therefore, we refer to the Bible with terms such as *God-breathed, inerrant,* and *infallible.*

Sometimes, I have enjoyed playing games with people. I once had a friend call the hotel where I was staying. When the phone in the room rang, I figured it was him. When I picked it up, I said "Front Desk." My friend asked for my room number. I told him that the room was now empty—the guest had already checked out that morning. My friend started getting nervous until I said, "How's it going, Brother!" For a moment, he thought he was hearing the voice of someone else. The point is, an eyewitness and an ear-witness are not always reliable! We have a more sure Word of prophecy.

Second, we notice the *method* of inspiration. In 2 Peter 1:21, the word *moved* carries the idea of being borne along or carried by the power of another. This same verb is used in Acts 27:15, where the wind determined the direction and destination of the boat. The sailors were completely controlled by the power of the wind and moved wherever the wind sent them. The word-picture the Holy Spirit is painting is that the *only* way for these men to have penned down God's Word was for the Spirit of God to carry or move them there. There was no way these men could reach this destination [of writing down inspired words] from their own efforts.

Preservation—God kept His Word.

The doctrine of preservation is based on the Bible itself. Since the Bible is to be our authority in matters of faith and practice, it is important to see what God has stated about its preservation for each generation.

> *"He hath remembered his covenant for ever, the word which he commanded to a thousand generations."*
> —Psalm 105:8

> *"For ever, O Lord, thy word is settled in heaven."*
> —Psalm 119:89

"Thy testimonies have I taken as an heritage for ever: for they are the rejoicing of my heart."—Psalm 119:111

"Thy word is true from the beginning: and every one of thy righteous judgments endureth for ever."—Psalm 119:160

"Heaven and earth shall pass away, but my words shall not pass away."—Matthew 24:35

"Being born again, not of corruptible seed, but of incorruptible, by the word of God, which liveth and abideth for ever. For all flesh is as grass, and all the glory of man as the flower of grass. The grass withereth, and the flower thereof falleth away: But the word of the Lord endureth for ever. And this is the word which by the gospel is preached unto you."—1 Peter 1:23–25 (This is a quotation from Isaiah 40, an indirect "proof" that this Scripture had already been preserved for over seven hundred years.)

There are seminaries that exist today that seem to "explain away" every verse that teaches preservation. I have a problem with someone who feels that verses or doctrine must be "explained away." I prefer to read the Bible and understand it literally. When God says His Word will last forever, that it will last for a thousand generations, I believe that means God will preserve His Word forever.

In the Bible, the writers had no problem quoting Scripture that had been preserved up to that time. Peter quotes Isaiah 40 (1 Peter 1:23–25); Paul quotes extensively from the Old Testament in Romans 9–11. Each time a New Testament writer quotes from the Old Testament, he is demonstrating that God has been able to preserve His Word. Preservation is highly debated today because ultimately, the preservation issue will decide the translation issue—and preservation is completely a matter of faith in God's power.

Illumination—God clarifies His Word.

> "But as it is written, Eye hath not seen, nor ear heard, neither have entered into the heart of man, the things which God hath prepared for them that love him. But God hath revealed them unto us by his Spirit: for the Spirit searcheth all things, yea, the deep things of God. For what man knoweth the things of a man, save the spirit of man which is in him? even so the things of God knoweth no man, but the Spirit of God. Now we have received, not the spirit of the world, but the spirit which is of God; that we might know the things that are freely given to us of God. Which things also we speak, not in the words which man's wisdom teacheth, but which the Holy Ghost teacheth; comparing spiritual things with spiritual. But the natural man receiveth not the things of the Spirit of God: for they are foolishness unto him: neither can he know them, because they are spiritually discerned. But he that is spiritual judgeth all things, yet he himself is judged of no man. For who hath known the mind of the Lord, that he may instruct him? But we have the mind of Christ."—1 Corinthians 2:9–16

Illumination is when God "turns the light on" for us on a certain passage. This process is a work that is done by the Holy Spirit, the writer and interpreter of Scripture. This is a present-tense type of work accomplished by the Spirit. Whereas inspiration was completed in the past, preservation began in the past and carries through today; illumination is for us today in the present.

Translation—God uses man to render His Word.

The process of translation occurs when someone takes a Hebrew Old Testament or a Greek New Testament and places those words into any other language. There are different philosophies involved in translating. It is possible to have a correct text, but a weak translation if the philosophy is not correct.

Some would view the translation process as purely an act of man. In some cases this is true. But, if you believe God preserves His Word, then you cannot separate Him completely from the rendering of His Word into other languages around the world. The promise of preservation requires that God use man to render accurate translations in other languages. This is often a strong dividing line among those with differing positions on this issue— did God preserve only the original languages and then leave His Word in the hands of men to render into other languages, or has His supernatural hand been involved in the preservation work throughout the translation process?

In addition, there are two approaches to translation: The New International Version is an example of a **dynamic equivalency** translation whereas the King James Version is an example of a **formal equivalency** translation. Dynamic equivalency means that translators have attempted to get the "concepts" and the meaning of one language into a receptor language. This involves much subjective interpretation by the translator. Formal equivalency means that the translator has attempted to go literally from word to word as much as the languages will allow.

DEFINING THE TERMS

Dynamic Equivalency: A process of translating used for the NIV and many other Bible translations that attempts to interpret and convey the intent of the message and thoughts of a source text rather than the literal words.

Formal Equivalency: also "verbal equivalency." A process of translation in which both the words and the forms of the words were rendered as closely as possible from Hebrew or Greek into English.

I once heard an antagonist to the King James position make a statement along these lines: "There is really no need to say, 'Let these sayings sink into your ears…,' when it is so much clearer to say, 'We need to listen carefully.'" I beg to differ. There indeed *is* a reason: these are the words that God has chosen; it is the way that God said it!

Granted there are times when the Greek or Hebrew may not be clear to us. If that is the case, we translate the words as they are and allow God to give illumination later. This is preferred over having one group of translators place their personal views into the translation. One translation committee wanted to use "popcorn" for "snow" because snow was unheard of in the region for which this Bible was intended. Another committee wanted to use "pig" for "Lamb of God" because the tribe did not know what a lamb was. As you can see, dynamic equivalency sounds good on the surface, but it opens the door for personal opinion regarding changes to God's Word.

Formal equivalency states that we translate what God said, then explain those words to those we are addressing. In this case, we use the word *lamb* and then teach the tribal people what a lamb is.

A high view of inspiration (i.e., a belief that God chose the exact words to give to each human writer) will necessitate high views of preservation and translation (i.e., we will do our best to get God's *words*, rather than His *concepts*, into every language possible).

Sometimes people ask the question, "Couldn't we update the Word of God and use *two* for the word *twain*?" Would we be changing the Word of God? It is possible to update God's Word without changing what God said. If it's not possible now, it would not have been possible in 1611. To change *twain* into *two* would not be changing what God said. In this case, we are not dealing with concepts, we are dealing with synonymous words. Yet, there is a more pressing question that must be answered first: Do we need a new translation? I do not believe so.

Friend, we have an accurate, literal translation (formal equivalency) of the Word of God from the right text in English.

Canonization—God's people recognize His Word.

Canonization is the term we use to describe how the books of the Bible came together as one volume or canon.

How did the Bible come together as we know it today? First, the prophets wrote the words of God. Exodus 24:4 says: "*And Moses wrote all the words of the LORD, and rose up early in the morning, and builded an altar under the hill, and twelve pillars, according to the twelve tribes of Israel.*"

The prophets wrote and were the recipients of this direct revelation. God gave them His Word. These precious words were kept. This is significant. The Old Testament Hebrew canon was kept meticulously by the Jews. The tribe of Levi was given the responsibility of being the keepers of the law. In Deuteronomy 31:26, the Bible says: "*Take this book of the law, and put it in the side of the ark of the covenant of the LORD your God, that it may be there for a witness against thee.*"

As the Old Testament books were written, God used three institutions to preserve His Word. First, He used the *home* as fathers were instructed in Deuteronomy 6:6–7: "*And these words, which I command thee this day, shall be in thine heart: And thou shalt teach them diligently unto thy children, and shalt talk of them when thou sittest in thine house, and when thou walkest by the way, and when thou liest down, and when thou risest up.*" Second, He used *spiritual leaders* as the priests and scribes were responsible to carefully copy and protect His Words. Third, He used the *government,* as kings were commanded to make their own copy of God's Word from the copies made by the priests and scribes (Deuteronomy 17:18).

Throughout the centuries, the books of the Old Testament were kept and propagated amongst God's people just as He commanded.

In Daniel 9:2 the Bible says: *"In the first year of his reign I Daniel understood by books the number of the years...."* Daniel was able to access the kept record. We begin to understand and receive a picture that the books were kept, acknowledged, known and added to, as God spoke to Daniel, Jeremiah, Micah and Malachi. The words of those who were known to be prophets of God were recorded and added to what we would call the canon of the Old Testament.

The time of the law and the prophets closed around 400 BC. From 400 BC until the New Testament, there was a period of silence. During that time the Apocrypha (a collection of Jewish historical books covering the time between the testaments) was written, but these books were never placed in the Jewish canon of scriptures, nor were they placed in the early church canon, for the simple fact that they were not written by the prophets. These books were not deemed as being inspired of God, but were deemed as merely historical accounts.

When the time came for the New Testament Church to recognize which books were inspired of God and which were not, there were several considerations used that were similar to those used to determine Old Testament canonization.

The first question asked concerning the New Testament books was simply, "Is this written by an apostle or someone who had direct contact with the apostles?" In other words, is there apostolic authority? The apostles were directly ordained by the Lord Jesus Christ for the purpose of spreading the truth. New Testament writers were either apostles or were directly influenced by the apostles, such as the case with Luke whom the Holy Spirit used to give us the books of Acts and the Gospel of Luke.

In Jude 17–18 the Bible says: *"But, beloved, remember ye the words which were spoken before of the apostles of our Lord Jesus*

Christ; How that they told you there should be mockers in the last time, who should walk after their own ungodly lusts."

Reading the twenty-seven books of the New Testament makes it obvious that the believers of the early church recognized this body of literature as being the inspired Word of God. In other words, Jude wasn't questioning what the apostles wrote. He was reminding the Christians in Asia Minor of what the apostles had already said.

The second consideration for the canonization of the New Testament was: were the writings in question consistent with the teachings of the Old Testament, Christ, and the apostles? The Bible says that Timothy knew the Scriptures from a child. This means that Timothy's mother and grandmother, Lois and Eunice, were women who knew the Old Testament. They read the Scriptures and taught Timothy of the coming of the Messiah. Faithful, godly men and women like Lois and Eunice were not going to receive New Testament writings that were inconsistent with the teachings of the Old Testament.

Enemies of the Bible (such as Dan Brown's best selling book, *The Da Vinci Code*) have said that the Bible, as we know it today, was collated by the Roman emperor, Constantine. These experts say that three hundred years after Christ, religious leaders "upgraded Jesus" to be the Son of God. They teach that prior to that time, there was no record of Jesus being called God's Son. This is simply not true. The Roman Catholic church did not give us the Scriptures or the deity of Christ. These doctrines and Scriptures were in place long before the fourth century.

The fact is that all twenty-seven books of the New Testament were written and received by the end of the first century. It is true that at the council of Carthage in 397 AD, there was the recognition of the twenty-seven books. They were formally recognized and canonized as being the books of the apostles. But all the council did in 397 was acknowledge what Christians had already acknowledged for centuries—that these books were truly the Word of God. By that time, this canon of twenty-seven books had already been functioning throughout the Christian population of the Mediterranean region. It had already been circulating since just after the last book was completed, around the end of the first century.

The third consideration of New Testament canonization was: are these letters authoritative in nature and is that authority of God?

The letters of the Apostle Paul were received immediately as being authoritative. In fact, many theological liberals today hate the books that were authored (in the human sense) by the Apostle Paul because they are so authoritative and to the point.

Occasionally, you may hear about "lost gospels" or supposed books of the Bible that were not included in the canon—such as the gospel according to Judas or the gospel according to Philip. These "lost gospels" have become props for those who seek to discredit the Christian faith. And many Christians wonder why they were not included in the Bible as we know it today.

In 1945, an Arabic peasant, digging in Egypt for fertilizer, found an earthenware container that held thirteen leather-bound papyrus books. These books dated from about 150 AD to about 400 AD and are known as the Gnostic Gospels. The word *Gnostic* comes from the Greek word *gnosis*, which means *knowledge*, but it also can mean *knowledge for those who have been enlightened*. These Gnostic Gospels are being presented by some historians as an "alternate canon"—equal to the Bible. Sadly, these Gnostic Gospels are becoming more and more accepted today by those who reject the true Word of God.

In addition, on Christmas Day in 2003, the History Channel aired a special claiming that the Apocryphal books should have been left in the canon of Scripture. The impression was given that they were banned from the canon because they promoted feminism.

Why were the Gnostic Gospels and the Apocryphal writings not placed into our hands and preserved to this day? There are several reasons of which you should be aware.

First, these writings were rejected because of the dates they were written. This is very simple but also very important. The Gnostic Gospel authors were not eyewitnesses of Jesus Christ. Even secular historians admit that these gospels were written between 150 AD and 400 AD. The earliest of the Gnostic Gospels was written 150 years after Christ, and others much later. There is no legitimate connection between these gospels and the first-century apostles. The Gnostics, trying to lend credibility to their writings, literally took the names of Christian people and falsely added them to their writings, hence the names "The Gospel of Thomas" or "The Gospel of Philip."

Second, the early Christians rejected these gospels because they were known to contain false teaching.

For example, these gospels pervert the doctrine of salvation. Gnostics believed that salvation was found in self-realization and that man did not need to be saved from sin. These gospels do not present Jesus as the Redeemer, and like the new-agers of today, Gnostics believed that we can all experience God in our own way.

Many twenty-first century authors and liberal theologians have an agenda that is anti-Christian—thus the Gnostic Gospels are very appealing. The Gnostic Bible is broad enough that you can essentially believe whatever you choose. There is no specific truth in the Gnostic Bible.

Time magazine, in an article entitled "The Lost Gospels" dated December 11, 2003, wrote: "The recovered text" (speaking of the Gnostic Gospels) "feeds America's ever sharpening appetite for mystical spirituality…[these gospels are] being accepted in today's climate by people who are disgruntled with church life."

These types of books are sometimes referred to as pseudo-epigraphical books, meaning fraudulent books or books that are false writings. There are hundreds of pseudo-epigraphical books from the first several centuries, including the Gnostic Gospels, that have never been received by true Christians in any century.

In short, the canon of Scripture as we know it today was assembled by the confirmation of God through the apostles and the faithful believers of the first century.

In his book *Protestant Christian Evidences*, Bernard Ramm writes:

> A thousand times over, the death knell of the Bible has been sounded, the funeral procession formed, the inscription cut on the tombstone, and committal read. But somehow the corpse never stays put. No other book has been so chopped, knifed, sifted, scrutinized, and vilified. What book on philosophy or religion or psychology or belles letters of classical or modern times has been subject to such a mass attack as the Bible—and with such venom and skepticism; with such thoroughness and erudition—upon every chapter, line and tenet? The Bible is still loved by millions, read by millions, and studied by millions.[2]

These foundational truths—inspiration, preservation, illumination, translation, and canonization—form the basis of our faith in the Word of God, the Bible.

Chapter Three In Summary

1. Inspiration is a Bible promise that applies to all Scripture and states that the words are literally God-breathed.

2. Preservation is a Bible promise that God is supernaturally involved in protecting and propagating His Word, not just inspiring it.

3. Illumination is the work of the Holy Spirit in your heart helping you to understand God's Word.

4. Translation is the efforts of men, hopefully under God's guidance, to transfer His words into another language.

5. Dynamic Equivalency is an effort by the translators to interpret the concepts rather than to translate the exact words. Modern translators have taken this approach.

6. Formal Equivalency is an effort by translators to create a literal word for word translation and leaves "interpretation" up to the reader. This was the approach of the King James translators.

7. Canonization refers to the efforts of the early Christians to recognize and bring the true Word of God into one volume, the Bible. During this process, many false books and letters were rejected.

8. All twenty-seven books of the New Testament were recognized by early Christians as God's Word by the end of the first century.

9. The Gnostic Gospels, because of their age and false doctrine, were rejected as "imposters" by early Christians.

CHAPTER FOUR

Understanding the Trouble

There is a great deal of trouble concerning the issues of biblical preservation and translations into different languages. Primarily, there are three areas that are "trouble-spots" when these twin issues are discussed. First and foremost, there is the trouble with doctrine. Second, there is the trouble of doubt. Finally, there is the trouble of division.

Trouble with Doctrine

I know that people who prefer the Critical Text often make statements such as, "There are no major doctrines affected with the new translations...." Yet, this statement is easily demonstrated as false. While many of the major doctrines are still found in newer versions, they are definitely affected by new wordings.

We are asserting that doctrine has primarily been diluted or "dumbed down," yet in many passages doctrines are actually changed or deleted altogether!

In the following examples, note the words in ***bold italic***. These important words are deleted from the Critical Text. Consider how these few examples weaken and dilute the doctrine of salvation:

*"And whosoever shall offend one of these little ones that believe **in me**, it is better for him that a millstone were hanged about his neck, and he were cast into the sea"* (Mark 9:42). Problem? Salvation is not simply about "belief." Rather, it is a particular belief in the Person of Jesus Christ.

*"Verily, verily, I say unto you, He that believeth **on me** hath everlasting life"* (John 6:47). Here again we encounter the same problem of salvation only being found in Jesus Christ.

*"Wherefore thou art no more a servant, but a son; and if a son, then an heir of God **through Christ**"* (Galatians 4:7). Here again we encounter a similar problem. The *only* way we can become a child of God and an heir of God is through Jesus Christ. To dilute this is to weaken the doctrine of salvation and to align more closely with the broad-road concept that all beliefs lead to Heaven, so long as you *really* believe.

*"In whom we have redemption **through his blood**, even the forgiveness of sins"* (Colossians 1:14). Failure to make mention of the blood of Christ is to ignore the principle of Hebrews 9:22, *"...and without shedding of blood is no remission."*

> *"And the nations **of them which are saved** shall walk in the light of it: and the kings of the earth do bring their glory and honour into it."*—REVELATION 21:24

David Sorenson in his book, *Touch Not the Unclean Thing*, writes regarding the above passages, "it should be apparent that the integrity of the doctrine of salvation through faith in Jesus Christ has been weakened. It has not been eliminated from the critical text, but it has been eroded."[1]

We could give additional information from the same source dealing with the doctrine of Christ being diluted. At times, His virgin birth is weakened (Matthew 1:25—note, in Critical Texts, "firstborn" is missing). His attribute of omnipresence is weakened in John 3:13 with the deletion of two simple words, "in heaven."

There is, however, at least one more doctrine that is affected by adhering to the philosophy of the Critical Text. Namely, if one believes that the Bible teaches the doctrine of preservation, then this biblical doctrine is greatly affected in the new translations.

It seems today that many times what the Scriptures say and what the scholars say do not always agree. For example, the Scriptures state the following truths:

> "Heaven and earth shall pass away, but my words shall not pass away."—MATTHEW 24:35

> "Thy word is true from the beginning: and every one of thy righteous judgments endureth forever."—PSALM 119:160

> "For ever, O LORD, thy word is settled in heaven."
> —PSALM 119:89

It sounds to me as though God is teaching us a doctrine of preservation. The Scriptures clearly teach that even if Heaven and earth were to pass away, the words would not. We are clearly taught that the righteous judgments of God endure forever, and that His Word has been forever settled in Heaven.

If you were to read many books on the translation issue today, it would not take you long before you came across statements from scholars (who many times are considered by mainstream evangelicalism to be conservative and orthodox) that contradict or explain away the clear teachings of Scripture. Here is what one seminary stated about the doctrine of preservation:

> While the Bible teaches the ultimate indestructibility of the verbal revelation of God (Matthew 24:35; 1 Peter 1:25), it does not tell us how and where the written manuscript lineage of that word is preserved. We believe that God

> has providentially preserved His Word in the many
> manuscripts, fragments, versions, translations, and
> copies of the Scriptures that are available and that by
> diligent study, comparison, and correlation, the original
> text (words) can be ascertained. We therefore hold that
> the integrity of any text type, translation, version, or
> copy of the Scriptures is to be judged by the autographs
> [original manuscript] only....[2]

There are some fair questions that must be addressed: Since we do not have the originals, how can we judge the copies? In other words, for someone to say that a particular verse is not found in the original autographs is making a statement that cannot be scientifically verified. Why? Because all of the originals were lost or destroyed within 100–200 years of writing!

For instance, there is no original manuscript of 1 Timothy 3:16. You would think that scholars on both sides of the issue would choose the reading that has the most manuscript evidence. The overwhelming textual evidence for the reading of 1 Timothy 3:16 is *"**God** was manifest in the flesh..."* rather than "**he** who was manifest...." The Critical Text advocate argues for the pronoun "he" rather than "God" based purely upon personal bias towards the evidence of **Codex Sinaiticus** and a few other manuscripts, in spite of the fact that even **Codex Vaticanus** has the other reading! This is one of the many places where Vaticanus and Sinaiticus disagree with each other, yet scholars chose the reading that weakens the doctrine of Christ's deity.

Yet, concerning this verse, the TR advocate will argue that the majority of Greek manuscripts contain the reading "God," that the **ancient versions** contained this reading, and that this reading has been recognized by Bible-believing churches throughout history.

So, is this simply an academic discussion about which manuscripts are more accurate? Are we attempting to reconstruct or restore the words of the original writers? Must history be our final authority? No. Concerning this verse (and the issue of Bible translations in general), the TR advocate has an advantage. Namely, he has the biblical doctrine of preservation and a large body of evidence supporting that reading and evidencing that God kept His promise.

Again, notice the quotation given on the previous page.

> …We believe that God has providentially preserved His Word in the many manuscripts, fragments, versions, translations, and copies of the Scriptures that are available and that by diligent study, comparison, and correlation, the original text (words) can be ascertained….

Based on this view, how can the Christian be sure that he has the right words—which ones did God preserve and which ones did over-zealous scribes add? Apparently he must diligently compare, correlate, and study the manuscripts, fragments, versions, translations, and copies of scriptures that are available. The statement made above sounds academic, theological, and spiritual, but it has no practical value to a searching Christian. The end of the logic, if you hold to that statement, is that, due to our endless comparisons and discovery, we cannot ever believe that we have the authoritative Word of God in English.

DEFINING THE TERMS

Codex Sinaiticus (Aleph or A): *A fourth century uncial manuscript of the Greek Bible, widely believed to be written between AD 330–350. (See expanded definition, p. 187.)*

Codex Vaticanus (B): *This manuscript has been housed in the Vatican Library for as long as it has been known, appearing in its earliest catalog of 1475 and in the 1481 catalog. Its place of origin and the history of the manuscript is uncertain. (See expanded definition, p. 187.)*

Ancient Versions: *In the textual issue, one looks not only at the Greek manuscripts, but also at what the believing churches were using in other languages. (See expanded definition, p. 196.)*

The primary basis for the Critical Text is two manuscripts named Vaticanus and Sinaiticus. How many Christians have ever been to the Vatican to see this ancient manuscript? This would be difficult since the Catholic church has prohibited its viewing. How many have been to the British Museum to see the Sinaiticus? How do you know that you have the Word of God without diligently comparing what you have against these "oldest and best" manuscripts? Furthermore, how many scholars do you know that have compared all 5,600 Greek manuscripts in order to be certain that they have all the words of God? Based on the aforementioned quote, no one can have a Bible with confidence.

Again, read the words from a leading scholar at a popular seminary:

> The doctrine of preservation of Scripture...is not a doctrine that is explicitly taught in Scripture, nor is it the belief that God has perfectly and miraculously preserved every word of the original autographs in one manuscript or text-type. It is a belief that God has providentially preserved His Word in and through all the extant manuscripts, versions, and other copies of Scripture... God has wonderfully and providentially preserved His Word in the multiplicity of extant manuscripts. *No passage of Scripture promises this,* but the evidence of history leaves no doubt that such is the case.[3]

There are serious problems with the logic that is used to come to such conclusions and with the obvious denial of a basic Bible promise. For example, we read that "no passage of Scripture promises" preservation. This is simply a false statement. All would agree that the originals were given by inspiration of God—there is no room for question or debate concerning inspiration. Again, we have no inspired originals today. Therefore, when someone states that we are to determine the accuracy of the copies we have based upon their correlation to the original autographs, we find ourselves in an indefensible position. The Bible can no longer be our final authority. Rather, we must look to God's working in history and to the expert opinions of scholars to validate our translations.

Those who would hold to the Critical Text position believe we can know by studying history that God has preserved His Word. Yet, how can one know by looking at history, when to begin with, no one knows what it looked like? There is no way that historical observation can give documented proof that nothing has been changed. This is against the laws of scientific observation. Our position on preservation must be a "faith-based" approach. Certainly, this is a watershed issue, but we must let the Bible speak for itself.

While I am not against scholarship or scholasticism, I am against scholarship being placed in authority over God's promises. Originally, the word *scholar* was a humble name to give someone. For example, *scholar* is used only twice in the Bible. In each instance (1 Chronicles 25:8 and Malachi 2:12), the word is used in contrast against a "master" or "teacher." The word literally means a "student," not a "teacher."

There is nothing wrong with working hard in order to understand an issue. To a certain extent, everyone depends on scholars for something, and thank God for Bible-believing scholars through the centuries who have held to the faith of Jesus Christ in purity and steadfastness. I know that I have personally benefited from the work of the scholars who were part of the Translation Committee for the King James Bible.

Having said that, I want to clarify something about scholarship. While scholasticism in and of itself is not evil, it is wrong to commit—to any individual or exclusive group—the determination of truth for every person in matters relating to faith. There is an important Baptist distinctive known as the "Priesthood of the Believers" which reminds us of each individual's responsibility to seek and know God's truth.

In addition, issues relating to the biblical text are matters of faith—regardless of which side of the issue one takes. Textual scholarship should not operate solely upon scientific principles as though there was nothing divine about the origin of our Bible. The Bible does have something to say about its own preservation, thus necessitating a doctrine of preservation.

Bible-believing Christians, whether ministers or laymen, must go about the process of identifying the correct biblical text within the context of the biblical doctrine of preservation. The question that must be answered is: For what will you trust the scholars, and which scholars will you trust? There have been some saints who were scholars, and there have been some scholars who were saints. These terms are compatible, but there have also been thousands of scholars through the centuries who were literally enemies of the Cross and of the truth of Jesus Christ—and many of them have been granted authority as textual critics by unsuspecting Christians.

While there is more to what the Bible says about its own preservation, enough has been given to demonstrate that those who take the Critical Text approach to the textual issue have to "explain away"—under the guise of scholarship—what the Bible clearly teaches.

For now, it is important to remember that not only is the doctrine of preservation diluted or deleted, but that there is also a subtle attack on doctrinal purity as well. Perhaps the best way to demonstrate this is with the following list.

I realize that we are only comparing one English translation against two others. I also understand that this list can be recreated to show the NASB (New American Standard Bible) or ESV (English Standard Version) as the standard and the KJV as the opponent. Yet, these three translations have been chosen deliberately as the NASB and ESV have become more popular among Bible believing Christians. Even with these inadequacies stated, I believe it is important to note the following truths:

1. The virgin birth is diluted or weakened when Joseph is made to be the father of Jesus.

> "And **Joseph** and his mother marvelled at those things which were spoken of him."—LUKE 2:33 (KJV)

> "And **His father** and mother were amazed at the things which were being said about Him."—LUKE 2:33 (NASB)

> "And **his father** and his mother marveled at what was said about him."—LUKE 2:33 (ESV)

2. The attributes of the deity of Christ are called into question by omitting a clear reference to the omnipresence of Christ.

> "And no man hath ascended up to heaven, but he that came down from heaven, even the Son of man **which is in heaven**."—JOHN 3:13 (KJV)

> "And no one has ascended into heaven, but He who descended from heaven, even the Son of Man."—JOHN 3:13 (NASB)

> "No one has ascended into heaven except he who descended from heaven, the Son of Man."—JOHN 3:13 (ESV)

3. The position we have in Christ is due to either the fact that we have placed our trust in Him or that we obey Him. If the NASB and ESV are correct, how many times are we allowed to "not obey" before the wrath of God abides on us again?

> "He that believeth on the Son hath everlasting life: and he that **believeth not** the Son shall not see life; but the wrath of God abideth on him."—JOHN 3:36 (KJV)

"He who believes in the Son has eternal life; but he who **does not obey** the Son shall not see life, but the wrath of God abides on him."—JOHN 3:36 (NASB)

"Whoever believes in the Son has eternal life; whoever **does not obey** the Son shall not see life, but the wrath of God remains on him."—JOHN 3:36 (ESV)

4. The proof of the Resurrection has been watered down. There is a vast difference between "infallible" and "convincing." People can be convinced of a lie, but something that is infallible is absolute truth.

*"To whom also he shewed himself alive after his passion by **many infallible proofs**, being seen of them forty days, and speaking of the things pertaining to the kingdom of God:"*—ACTS 1:3 (KJV)

"To these He also presented Himself alive, after His suffering, by **many convincing proofs**, appearing to them over a period of forty days, and speaking of the things concerning the kingdom of God."—ACTS 1:3 (NASB)

"He presented himself alive to them after his suffering by **many proofs**, appearing to them during forty days and speaking about the kingdom of God."—ACTS 1:3 (ESV)

5. In 1 Timothy 3:16, another attempt is made by some of the modern translations to weaken the deity of Christ. *You and I* are "manifest in the flesh"—and we have both "appeared in a body" (these are the wordings used in the NIV). So what? There is nothing special about a person having a body. Yet, it is something unique that God came to earth as a man or that *"God was manifest in the flesh"* (as the KJV states).

6. Finally, the doctrine of the Trinity has been watered down. In one of the clearest passages in the Bible on this doctrine, new translations, based on Egyptian manuscripts, are lacking 1 John 5:7. Even though this verse was quoted by **Cyprian**, an early church leader in about 250 AD (at least 100 years "older" than any manuscript from Egypt not having the verse), it is still questioned or left out of Bibles derived from the Critical Text.

> *"For there are three that bear record in heaven, the Father, the Word, and the Holy Ghost: and these three are one."*—1 JOHN 5:7 (KJV)

> *"And it is the Spirit who bears witness, because the Spirit is the truth."*—1 JOHN 5:7 (NASB)

> *"For there are three that testify:"*—1 JOHN 5:7 (ESV)

While a complete defense of this verse is outside of the scope of this book, suffice it to say, this verse has evident support from the Latin manuscripts (which actually outnumber the Greek manuscripts) and can be shown to be accepted by Bible-believing

NOTABLE NAMES

Cyprian: *He was bishop of Carthage and an important early Christian writer. He was probably born at the beginning of the third century in North Africa, perhaps at Carthage, where he received an excellent classical (pagan) education. After converting to Christianity, he became a bishop (AD 249) and eventually died a martyr at Carthage. Important in the area of textual debate is that he quotes from 1 John 5:7.*

Tertullian: *From North Africa (probably Carthage—155–225), he was a Christian apologist and writer, one of the first to write extensively in Latin. Around 195, he converted to Christianity from Paganism. Tertullian was the first to use the term Trinitas (trinity) to describe the Godhead. In so doing, he paved the way for the development of orthodox Trinitarian and Christological doctrines. (See expanded definition, p. 193.)*

churches within one-hundred years of the apostles. For example, **Tertullian** referred to this verse in his writings.

It is hard to say that new translations are simply updating the archaic words or making it easier to read with examples like these. To me, it is easy to understand, *"these three are one."* These words are not so complicated that they need to be left out! In the Critical Text translations we find many problems with doctrine: the doctrine of preservation is removed and other important doctrines of the Christian faith are seriously compromised.

Similar types of concerns arise with every new English translation available on the market today. The New King James Version is widely accepted as the "closest translation" to the King James. Yet, a quick comparative study reveals serious questions about this new version. Notice the important translational differences in the following verses:

*"Be ye **followers** of me, even as I also am of Christ."*
—1 Corinthians 11:1 (KJV)

"**Imitate** me, just as I also **imitate** Christ."
—1 Corinthians 11:1 (NKJV)

*"And to her was granted that she should be arrayed in fine linen, clean and white: for the fine linen is the **righteousness** of saints."*—Revelation 19:8 (KJV)

"And to her it was granted to be arrayed in fine linen, clean and bright, for the fine linen is the **righteous acts** of the saints."—Revelation 19:8 (NKJV)

*"For as ye in times past have **not believed** God, yet have now obtained mercy through their **unbelief**: Even so have these also now **not believed**, that through **your mercy** they also may obtain mercy."*
—Romans 11:30–31 (KJV)

"For as you were once **disobedient** to God, yet have now obtained mercy through their **disobedience**, even so these also have now been **disobedient**, that through the mercy shown you they also may obtain mercy."
—ROMANS 11:30–31 (NKJV)

"For the preaching of the cross is to them that perish foolishness; but unto us which **are saved** it is the power of God."—1 CORINTHIANS 1:18 (KJV)

"For the message of the cross is foolishness to those who are perishing, but to us who **are being saved** it is the power of God."—1 CORINTHIANS 1:18 (NKJV)

"For what if some did not believe? shall their unbelief make the **faith** of God without effect?"—ROMANS 3:3 (KJV)

"For what if some did not believe? Will their unbelief make the **faithfulness** of God without effect?"
—ROMANS 3:3 (NKJV)

I realize that some claim these to be *translational* decisions not textual. Yet, the fact remains that when looking at these verses, Christians of today are left wondering which is correct. Has our English Bible been wrong for the last 360 years until a new team of translators finally got it right? If not, then why make the changes at all? Are these changes made merely for the sake of "variety"? If so, this is a weak reason to alter the Word of God.

In addition to these few comparisons, there are other problems with this translation. First, a completely different Old Testament text was used. Second, the pronouns of this version are less precise than the King James. Third, the footnotes continually refer the reader to the Critical Text. Fourth, there are many other translational differences that hold great significance for the discerning Christian. The New King James completely retranslates the sin of "sodomy" to "perverted one," it retranslates "hell" to the Greek word "hades," and the list goes on. In each of these translational differences, there is a subtle shift away from more clear and definitive Bible words. And fifth, the New King James committee chose a greater degree of dynamic equivalency and departed from the Received Text in a number of cases.

The case strengthens when we consider that the original words in the King James Version were chosen by a more qualified team of translators in a more detailed process of translation.

Granted, these examples have been a brief overview and could be reasoned away as *translational preferences*. Yet, these changes certainly open up believers to the doubt and doctrinal uncertainty that is common among Critical Text supporters, and the changes have not been proven necessary when compared against the Received Text.

Jude told the first-century believers that they were to *"contend for the faith"* (the body of beliefs) that had been *"once delivered"* (with the implication that these beliefs would not be delivered again) *"unto the saints."* Our generation stands in danger of allowing part of our body of beliefs to be eroded unless we stand and confront the trouble with doctrine lacking in most new translations.

Trouble with Doubt

If the former problems were not enough to at least alert you, there are also problems of doubt that arise from the use of the modern translations. There are at least three areas of the Scriptures that are called into question: 1) the accuracy of the Scriptures, 2) the availability of the Scriptures, and 3) the assurance of the Scriptures.

Consider again the statement we saw earlier made by Jesus in John 7:8 as it is compared with other modern translations:

KJV: *"Go ye up unto this feast: I go not up **yet** unto this feast; for my time is not yet full come."*

ESV: *"You go up to the feast. I am not going up to this feast, for my time has not yet fully come."*

NASB: *"Go up to the feast yourselves; I do not go up to this feast because My time has not yet fully come."*

The difference here is subtle. In the Received Text, Jesus is not going up *yet*. In the Critical Text, He is not going *at all*. Yet, later on in the chapter, *He goes*. If Jesus states unequivocally, "I am not going…" and then goes, He is a liar. On the other hand, if He states, "I am not going yet…" and then shows up, He has not been deceptive. In this example, the One Who is Truth (John 14:6) is placed in an indefensible position in the Critical Text and modern translations. We can easily see how doubt rather than faith could overtake a group Bible study of this passage.

Another problem of doubt that stems from the use of modern Bibles is the doubt cast upon the availability of Scriptures. Imagine that you are in a church setting. The preacher, who is reading from a King James Bible, says to turn in your Bibles to Acts 8:37. Imagine you are trying to follow along with him in a New American Standard Bible. Finally, you are able to find the passage. This particular verse is relegated to a footnote at the bottom of the page and is not in the text. This story would be repeated if you were asked to turn to John 8:1–11 to read the story of the woman caught in adultery. In Matthew 17:21, Matthew 18:11, and Mark 16:9–20 you would find that the NASB and the NIV have these verses either not appearing at all, or they are placed in brackets or in a footnote with an explanation stating that these verses do not appear in the "best" and oldest manuscripts.

These are just a few of the scores of verses that are missing from the Critical Text, and subsequently from the translations that descend from it. When a layman reads statements like, "This verse is not found in the best manuscripts," doubt is placed in his mind as to the availability of Scripture. Also, the question of these being the "best" manuscripts is a biased statement that is highly in question by those who study the facts. We will understand more about these manuscripts in another chapter.

Within this context of "doubt," we also find a lack of assurance of the Scriptures. Gordon Fee stated that no two manuscripts anywhere in existence are exactly alike.[4]

Here is a similar quote from another "authority" on the subject: "…He [God] has preserved His Word in and through the thousands of extant manuscripts and that *those who seek truth must compare those manuscripts* to determine the correct readings when the manuscripts differ."[5]

I want a Bible that is available and trustworthy. I do not have the access nor the time to compare thousands of manuscripts to determine God's Word. For that matter, neither does the rest of Christendom!

We must continue in the things which we have learned as well as continuing in those things which the early church received. What the church received as Scripture was accurate, available, and commanded their full assurance. God's Word was made for the common man (the ploughboy of **Tyndale's** day). It was not hid for the scholars to find and restore for us. The Word of God deserves our explicit trust—man is prone to error no matter how sincere he may be.

Trouble with Division

Finally, as we consider the problems found in new translations, we must remember that it is not only the troubles of doctrine and doubt, but also a trouble of division.

To be sure, this issue is divisive. There has been much written on this subject and there will be much more to follow. This debate has been raging for at least fifty years in America. It polarizes churches, hinders missionaries from reaching the field, and makes enemies out of people who are part of our spiritual family. The speech accompanying this issue is not always filled with grace. Rather, many times with this subject there is an inability to "speak the truth in love." It appears at times that if two people cannot agree on this issue they are destined to be mortal enemies until the rapture!

First, this issue causes a trouble of division because of position. Too many people have branded those with differing views as "non-Bible-believers" or "heterodox."

There are those who take such an extreme position on the "King James only" side of the debate that anyone who disagrees with them is branded an idiot. When the majority of people hear the words "King James only," they automatically tend to lump every King James Bible supporter into this group. This is an untruthful stereotype.

However, those from the King James side are not alone in their divisive speech. This quote from Larry Pettegrew insightfully demonstrates how those trained in the Critical school think: "The King James only [he does not define this term] position is based on a heterodox view of the inspiration and preservation of the Bible and is, consequently, *non-fundamentalist* and *non-evangelical* [emphasis added]."[6]

Is Larry Pettegrew claiming that those who believe the Word of God is preserved in the Textus Receptus and that the King James Bible is an accurate translation of that body of truth are not fundamental? Compare his statement with the view of Professor Robert Gromacki, of Cedarville University. Gromacki, in his book,

NOTABLE NAMES

William Tyndale: *He was the first to translate the Bible into English from a Greek (Byzantine) source. Nearly 90% of his work is still retained in the King James Bible. He lived from 1494–1536, and died as a martyr for translating the Bible for the common man.*

New Testament Survey, admits that the Authorized Version is the Bible of Fundamentalism.[7]

Edward Glenny raises the rhetoric to another level when he says, "Some proponents of the Traditional Text claim its superiority and the satanic character of all other text types by ignoring much of the evidence concerning the text of the New Testament. They are *cultic* in this regard."[8]

Based on the two quotations from the book put forth by a Baptist seminary, here is what I learn about myself: First, I am a "non-fundamentalist" and a "non-evangelical" because I believe that God preserved His Word for every generation through Bible-believing churches, and because I believe the King James is a translation that reflects that heritage and tradition (hence, the Traditional Text).

Furthermore, I learn that I am now "heterodox" in my belief concerning the doctrine of preservation. This is ironic, for if there is no such thing as a "Bible doctrine of preservation," one can neither be "orthodox" or "heterodox." To call someone "heterodox" belies the fact that those of the opposite opinion must concede that preservation is a Bible doctrine.

Not only am I no longer a fundamentalist or evangelical, and heterodox in my belief, I find that I am also cultic in my thinking. This type of speech, regardless of which side of the issue it comes from, will inevitably lead to division. Those who are characterized by this type of thinking and speech, regardless of which side they take, have a problem with their attitude.

I want to have charity and grace enough to state that someone who disagrees with the position of this book could still be a biblical fundamentalist. Godly men may disagree and yet still be greatly used of the Lord.

I do not attempt to make enemies in this debate by unfairly slandering those who do not agree with my position. We must remember who the real enemy is—Satan. We must remember that contending for the faith is more than simply contending for the "book" in which that faith is found. We must remember that "marking those who cause division" is not the same as "marking those who don't see eye-to-eye" with me on every issue.

There is also a division caused by practice of good men. Paul states in 1 Corinthians 14:8, *"For if the trumpet give an uncertain sound, who shall prepare himself to the battle?"* Imagine the confusion existing in the average churches that believe any Bible will do! What happens when someone preaches from the last half of Mark 16, but half the congregation does not have that in their Bibles? What will happen when the visiting speaker defends the orthodox belief of the Trinity from 1 John 5:7, and someone with a Revised Version does not even have this verse in the footnotes? If someone is going to believe that the Critical Text is better and the best translation from that text is the NASB, that person would do well to consistently employ that version throughout his church for the sake of unity and public reading.

I do not think the problems brought on by the Bible controversy can be overstated. Everywhere we turn we see apostasy running rampant even in the midst of what used to be mainstream Christianity. God's anointing power in preaching has been lost because men have become critics of God's Word. We are wasting our time as self proclaimed "Bible scavenger hunters"—seeking hidden or lost truth by comparing version with version or by digging into corrupt sources when the truth and the power of God is right in our hands for the taking!

Men are no longer trembling at God's Word and humbling themselves before it. We are no longer allowing the Word of God to inspect us, but rather we have become word inspectors!

More could be said about the trouble experienced through the Bible version controversy. This chapter has only provided a highlight of the many doctrinal questions and problems that have arisen due to wording changes in modern versions. Much more could be said about the doubt that this issue casts upon the Christian faith, even in the minds of lost men who wonder "why so many Bibles?" And it is obvious that multiplicity of modern Bibles has weakened our fellowship as believers, our fervency as His ambassadors, and our witness to the lost world.

CHAPTER FOUR IN SUMMARY

1. The new Critical Text leaves out many words that are essential to the foundational doctrines of the Christian faith.

2. Our position on preservation must be "faith-based."

3. Not all Bible-scholars are Bible-believing scholars.

4. New versions diminish the following doctrines: the virgin birth, the deity of Christ, salvation, the resurrection, the trinity, and others.

5. New translations have gone far beyond updating archaic words.

6. New versions have cast doubt upon entire verses and passages of Scripture that are historically supported by many witnesses.

7. The Bible debate has divided Christians and has brought about harsh speech and arrogant attitudes.

8. Lost men, in need of Christ, wonder "why so many Bibles?"

Understanding the Truth

In John 17:17, while praying for us, Jesus makes a statement that is foundational to our view of the Bible. He said, *"Sanctify them through thy truth: thy word is truth."* Again, in John 17:8, Jesus states, *"For I have given them the words which thou gavest me; and they have received them...."*

As we prepare to see the truth about the textual and preservation issues, we need to observe two principles from the verses above in John 17. First, the words Jesus gave are the *only source* of absolute truth. Second, the words He gave were *received* by the early church. Jesus, the Founder, Builder, and Head of the church called unto Himself the twelve apostles (Matthew 10:1–5). These men, personally equipped by Christ, were the early leaders (Christ Himself being the Chief Cornerstone) of the church (Ephesians 2:20). This church was not only established by Christ during His earthly ministry, but also it was equipped to do the work of the ministry. This equipping was through His received words (John 17:17; 2 Timothy 3:17; Ephesians 4:11–16).

We have noticed already statements made by scholars instructing us that the Bible does not teach preservation. Yet, as Bible believers, we have a responsibility to test this statement against the Scripture itself. The truth, when compared against what the Word of God actually states, is that the Bible teaches explicitly and implicitly that He will preserve His Word and that men should live by that Word.

Before we look at what Scripture teaches us, it is necessary to define the position of the scholars. As already noted, the word *scholar* is not a bad word. Originally, it meant a student, a learner—not a master or authority. Yet, in the realm of scholarship today, there are four critical positions that affect the paradigm of truth.

First, there is the position of the theological liberal. A theological liberal is characterized by the word *unbelief.* He does not believe in the resurrection, the deity of Christ, nor the authority of the Scriptures. Within the context and scope of this book, the liberal is not the one being addressed. He will not hear Scripture. In the textual/translational debate, fundamentalists are not addressing the liberal crowd. For the liberal, it is not "Which translation contains the most correct reading of God's Word?" Rather, for him, God's Word cannot be found today.

Second, there is the position of the neo-orthodox. This person is characterized by the term *unbelief disguised.* He has attributed a different meaning to key terms so that he sounds like he is a believer. If asked about the resurrection, he may say that he believes in it. Yet, if he is pushed further, you will find that he believes in a "spiritual" resurrection. If asked about his position on Jesus being the Son of God, he gladly concurs that Jesus is the Son of God, "as we are all sons of God." If asked about his position on the Bible and its authority, he seems orthodox until you find that the Bible is his authority as he interprets it (which makes him his own authority). We will briefly look at a few statements from those of this persuasion as they apply to the textual/translational issue.

Third, there is the position of the new-evangelical. This group of people, which developed in the 1940s, was known in its early days as the *Intellectual Fundamentalist*. This person is characterized by the term *belief compromised*. He wants to dialogue with the liberal and neo-orthodox crowd in an attempt to draw them to his position. However, what has happened is that he becomes more like them. While the fundamentalist emphasizes separation, the new evangelical emphasizes infiltration. Here is one evangelical's concern for where compromised belief leads:

> The faith-world of John Wesley, Jonathan Edwards, John Jay, William Wilberforce, Hannah Moore, Lord Shaftesbury, Catherine Booth, Hudson Taylor, D.L. Moody, Charles Spurgeon, Oswald Chambers, Andrew Murray, Carl Henry, and John Stott is disappearing. In its place a new evangelicalism is arriving in which therapeutic self-concern overshadows knowing God, spirituality displaces theology, end-times escapism crowds out day-to-day discipleship, marketing triumphs over mission, references to opinion polls outweigh reliance on biblical exposition, concerns for power and relevance are more obvious than concern for piety and faithfulness, talk of reinventing the church has replaced prayer for revival, and the characteristic evangelical passion for missionary enterprise is overpowered by the all-consuming drive to sustain the multiple business empires of the booming evangelical subculture.[1]

Finally, at the far end of the spectrum is the fundamentalist. He is characterized by the word *belief*. There is no discussion needed. If the Bible makes a statement, it is to be believed rather than re-interpreted or doubted.

Simply defining these terms is not enough. Rather, we need to look at the writings of key individuals to notice what some of these positions really teach. Sometimes, it is not "what they say," as much as it is "what they do not say" that characterizes each position.

Neo-Orthodox Position

These quotes are from men who, today, would be considered neo-orthodox in their theology. They are at times very technical. Yet, as one places these statements under the light of biblical Christianity, problems surface.

> In the fourth century, mixture prevailed almost everywhere: Nearly all its texts, so far as they can be seen through the quotations of theologians, are more or less chaotic. In the early years, the persecution under Diocletian and his colleagues, and then the reaction under Constantine, must have affected the text not less powerfully than the Canon of the New Testament.[2]

What is the problem with this statement? What do these statements mean? The first quote implies that there was only confusion and chaos. This statement, given as a dogmatic "must" is based on assumption, not Scripture. The assumption from history is that the persecution of Diocletian starting in 303 AD powerfully affected the text of Scripture. This cannot be verified or historically observed. What are we to do when it "appears" that something historically may not line up with the Scriptures. We rest in the authority of Scriptures! History will ultimately catch up to the Bible. Scripture has stated that God's Word is eternal (Isaiah 40:8; 1 Peter 1:25; Psalm 111:7–8).

> When the Western text was growing up…the reverence paid to the writings which ultimately formed the Canon of New Testament had not yet assumed a character that would forbid what might well seem their temperate enrichment from other memories or records.[3]

Again, we find assumptions. This quote implies that the Word of God was not reverenced as such. These early Christians were being taught the Word of God which had explicit warnings (in both testaments) of either deleting or adding to it. To assume that a scribe or copyist "enhanced" the text from his memory alone is to assume that the early Christians did not have a high regard for God's Word—a thought that is easily dismissed when one studies how many gave their lives for the Book.

The presumption that the copyist had the liberty to add things that they felt would "enrich" the passage is another glaring problem. When dealing with copying large portions of Scripture, the more common mistake was not adding something, but would have been deleting or skipping over something—and this would have been a very rare mistake given the scribal process. It is hard to believe that someone just "added" the last twelve verses of Mark and that this addition found its way into the Received Text of the entire Byzantine empire! It would be much more likely that the scribe of the obscure Vaticanus and Siniaticus manuscripts left it out (further explaining why these inaccurate manuscripts landed in obscurity). It is also important to note that these two manuscripts that form the essence of the Critical Text disagree between themselves more than 5,000 times in the Gospels alone.

Many writers also divide the manuscript evidence into several text-families (called Stemmatics), such as **Byzantine, Alexandrian,** etc.

DEFINING THE TERMS

Byzantine Greek Text: *A synonym for the Received Text notating that it flowed throughout that Byzantine Empire, which historically correlates with early missionary efforts and apostolic writings of the first century.*

Alexandrian manuscripts: *These manuscripts are dated to the fourth century. They originated in Alexandria, Egypt. They are Byzantine in the Gospels, Alexandrian in the Epistles. These manuscripts are in question by Bible-believers because of the false "Alexandrian" teachings that influenced their textual readings.*

Fenton John Anthony Hort, one of the developers of the Critical Text believed that this Western Text was mostly a paraphrase by its editors. (We will cover more about his beliefs in chapter seven.) He states:

> Words, clauses, and even whole sentences were changed, omitted, and inserted with astonishing freedom, wherever it seemed that the meaning could be brought out with greater force and definiteness.... Another equally important characteristic is a disposition to enrich the text at the cost of its purity by alterations or additions taken from traditional and perhaps from apocryphal or other non-bibical sources.... Another impulse of scribes abundantly exemplified in Western readings is the fondness for assimilation.... But its most dangerous work is "harmonistic" corruption, that is, the partial or total obliteration of differences in passages otherwise more or less resembling each other.[4]

Again, these statements are not factual, but assumptions that fit the theory of an "evolving" text. The statements made by Mr. Hort became the foundation for the principle that the "shortest reading is to be preferred."

> But it is at least theoretically possible that the originality of the text thus attained is relative only, and that all existing documents are affected by errors introduced in the early stages of transmission.[5]

This quote implies that there were mistakes made early in the process of transmission, which means that the true text was not preserved, but restored, based on the two oldest manuscripts. To clarify, these scholars are assuming that shortly after the time of Christ and the writings of these Scriptures, the whole process broke down! Somehow it all fell apart and from that point forward the true Word of God became a mystery that must be continually mined and revised. This is not a belief in preservation, but rather restoration. Which do you believe is more biblical—preservation or restoration?

> Wherever it has appeared to the editors, or to either of them, that the text probably contains some primitive error, that it has not been quite rightly preserved in any existing document....[6]

Westcott and Hort believed that no existing document correctly preserves God's Word. In other words, God gave some words which are not to be found anywhere. How can you know this scientifically? This is a presupposition based upon personal bias. Do not these quotes betray an agenda on the part of Westcott and Hort to undermine the Received Text? Here is a statement from Hort:

> ...I had no idea till the last few weeks of the importance of texts, having read so little Greek Testament. ...and dragged on with the villainous Textus Receptus.... Think of that vile Textus Receptus leaning entirely on late manuscripts; it is a blessing there are such early ones.[7]

From the beginning, the men behind the Critical Text were heavily biased against the Received Text, the one that the King James translators preferred with good reason. And their claims that their manuscripts are older simply do not hold up when considering the fact that Scripture readings that match the Received Text date back to the first-century church in early versions (e.g., The **Old Latin** and Syriac Peshitta) as well as in the writings of early church leaders.

DEFINING THE TERMS

Old Latin (Italic): *The Bible used by early Latin Christians, primarily Waldensians, a group of Christians persecuted by the organized Roman church. It is referred to as "old" because the Catholic church rejected it for the Latin Vulgate.*

The discovery of Vaticanus and Sinaiticus did not bring as much new information to the table as scholars would have you to believe. This discovery merely provided a smoke screen for secretive and biased revising of the Scriptures, unquestioningly settled many centuries before.

New-Evangelical Position

William Ashbrook, on page 3 of his book *Evangelicalism: The New Neutralism*, writes that there are four valid reasons for Christians to avoid the philosophy of Neo-Evangelicalism. "First, it is a movement born of compromise. Second, it is a movement nurtured in pride of intellect. Third, it is a movement growing on appeasement of evil; and finally it is a movement doomed by the judgment of God's Holy Word...."[8]

John Ashbrook, the son of the first writer, expounded his father's thesis in *New Neutralism II: Exposing the Gray of Compromise*. It is his conviction that there are three primary dangers associated with having belief compromised. "First, new evangelicalism determined to reject biblical separation. Second, new evangelicalism determined to find acceptance by the world. Third, new evangelicalism determined to add the social gospel to the scriptural gospel."[9]

Dr. Harold John Ockenga has been called "the Father of New Evangelicalism." When the National Association of Evangelicals was born in 1942, its first President was Harold John Ockenga. As a pastor, he occupied the pulpit of Park Street Congregational Church on the edge of Boston Common. When Fuller Theological Seminary was founded in 1947, its first President was Dr. Harold John Ockenga. *Christianity Today*, a major publication of new evangelicalism, had its birth in 1956 as the brainchild of Billy Graham and his father-in-law, Dr. L. Nelson Bell. The Chairman of the Board of the new magazine was Dr. Harold John Ockenga. When the World Congress on Evangelism convened in 1966, one of the three featured speakers was Dr. Harold John Ockenga. In the history of new evangelicalism, there is no more important name than that of Dr. Harold John Ockenga.

I don't wish to give a strictly negative caricature of Dr. Ockenga, who passed away in 1985. He was a conservative Presbyterian theologian who followed Dr. J. Gresham Machen's exodus from Princeton to Westminster Seminary. Yet, I believe his own words will speak volumes for his position:

> Neo-evangelicalism was born in 1948 in connection with a convocation address which I gave in the Civic Auditorium in Pasadena. While reaffirming the theological view of fundamentalism, this address repudiated its ecclesiology and its social theory. The ringing call for a repudiation of separatism and the summons to social involvement received a hearty response from many evangelicals.... It differed from fundamentalism in its repudiation of separatism and its determination to engage itself in the theological dialogue of the day. It had a new emphasis upon the application of the gospel to the sociological, political, and economic areas of life.[10]

Ockenga stated that "his ringing call" was a repudiation of separatism. In other words he opposed the biblical doctrine of separation and emphasized a much more social gospel. He had a philosophy that involved "infiltrating" the ranks of the Neo-Orthodox and winning them to his position. Yet, this is a clear violation of 2 Corinthians 6:17–18, Ephesians 5:11, and is the theme of 2 John.

The foundation of this "theology" was built with a pragmatic view to evangelism, rather than a scriptural view. With the scriptural foundations eroded, future generations of new evangelicals would have no clear and final scriptural authority. The results of this position are clear today, as we see a new generation of Christians who exhibit a lifestyle and world view that is in no way different from the unsaved world. The philosophy of "infiltration" ultimately became "seeker-sensitive" evangelism—and it has failed to produce a Christianity that is more biblical and distinct. Many, even within the ranks of the "seeker-sensitive" movement, are beginning to admit the failure of their carnal approach to worship.

Consider the statements made by George Ladd, a contemporary of Ockenga:

> ...the truth of infallibility does not extend to the preservation of an infallible text, nor to an infallible lexicography, nor to infallible answers to all questions about authorship, date, sources, etc, nor to an infallible reconstruction of the historical situation in which revelatory events occurred and the books of the Bible were written. Such questions God in His providence has committed to human scholarship to answer; and often the answers must be imperfect and tentative.[11]

> God inspired the authors of the Bible to produce a divinely superintended record; He has committed the reproduction and the preservation of the text to the vagaries of human history [not to the church]; and the establishment of a trustworthy text is the labor of scientific scholarship.[12]

These statements by George Ladd are not the statements of an ignorant man. Ladd was highly qualified with an intelligent mind. Yet, to an "intellectual fundamentalist," sometimes scholarship seems to be more important than Scripture. All answers that come from human scholarship will be imperfect and tentative—this is why we need an Absolute Scripture! Based on Ladd's quotes, we must ultimately trust the scholarship of human understanding rather than the promises of Scripture that have been passed down through generations. Where does any Christian get the idea that God "has committed the reproduction and the preservation of the text to the vagaries of human history"? Scripture clearly teaches us otherwise!

In Matthew 4:4, we are commanded to live by every Word of God, yet we learn from Ladd that these words are imperfectly preserved through the vagaries of human history. Only scholarship can restore us the correct text—and that apparently is a never-ending process. Again, it is easy to see that the foundation here is a belief in the need to *restore* the Scriptures rather than a belief that Scripture has already been *preserved*.

Os Guiness painfully observes that "signs are that, unless some drastic rethinking takes place soon, the corruptions in evangelicalism will worsen and show through in theology, not just in practice. Evangelicals have followed the broader cultural shift from 'religion to spirituality' and in the process have become chronically individualistic rather than corporate; they have become 'do-it-yourself' in their preferences rather than living under authority...."[13]

Over time, a believer who wants to appeal to the intellectualism of the day will compromise so often that he will start to sound and believe more like the liberal than the fundamentalist.

Non-KJV Fundamentalist Position

As stated already, while even some new evangelicals recognize the King James Bible to be the Bible of fundamentalism, one does not necessarily have to hold to the superiority of the King James over other Bibles to be a fundamentalist. By the term *fundamentalist*, I am referencing the historical context in which that "label" came to be embraced. The original formulation for what came to be called "fundamentalism" can be traced back to the Niagara Bible Conferences of 1878–1897. In 1910, at the General Assembly of the Presbyterian Church, these five fundamentals became the distinguishing marks against the modernists:

1. Inerrancy of Scripture
2. Virgin Birth and Deity of Christ
3. Vicarious Atonement of Christ

4. Bodily Resurrection of Christ
5. Visible Return of Christ

In the following quotations, we find leading men, claiming to hold to the fundamentals of the faith, express their opinions concerning the translation issue:

> We do not hold that the Word of God is to be found exclusively in one English translation or any one translation in any other language since all such have mis-translations, mis-copying, or mis-printing, however minor, and are not therefore inerrant.[14]

The doctrine of inerrancy means that the Bible has correctly recorded an event, conversation, battle, etc.—as it happened. It is a confusion of terms to state that we cannot have an inerrant copy. Jesus commanded those of His day to *"Search the scriptures; for in them ye think ye have eternal life..."* (John 5:39). He believed and taught that their *copies* were correct and inerrant.

Furthermore, there is a logical inconsistency with the statement given. If the Word of God is not to be found exclusively in one translation, then the logical conclusion would be that either they all contain the Word of God, or they all contain "part" of it. If they all contain the Word of God, what do you do when someone's Bible does not have the last twelve verses of Mark? If every Bible must be diligently compared because we do not have an authoritative Bible, how can we preach with authority? If God promised to magnify His Word above His own name (Psalm 138:2), then how has the church "lost" this exalted Word through her history?

One author writes:

> We gladly affirm God's providential control over the events of history so that His Word has been preserved by natural processes in the many extant manuscripts, versions, and other copies of the Scripture.[15]

This statement assumes preservation is based upon *natural* processes rather than *supernatural*. Preservation is based upon the promises and power of the Lord Jesus Christ. This writer continues:

> Therefore, instead of saying that God has preserved His Word in any one text or edition, as the TR/Majority Text advocates argue, it is better to say He has preserved His Word in and through the thousands of extant manuscripts, and that those who seek truth must compare those manuscripts to determine the correct readings when the manuscripts differ.[16]

This same writer also states: "…the New Testament context also indicates that it is speaking of the infallibility and incorruptible nature of the Word of God and not of the preservation of the text of Scripture." This quote, which deals with the verse of 1 Peter 1:23–25, makes a distinction between God's Word and the "text of Scripture." This is a rather bizarre, nebulous approach to Scripture. In other words, the Word of God is infallible in some ethereal and vague way, but not the actual text that records the words. Is not the "text" God's Word? If not, where is God's Word to be found?

These statements imply a logical impossibility. There is no way to judge the present copies by a non-existent autograph to determine its accuracy. There is no way to compare the textual words to some formless, intangible "word." For these positions, preservation is a possibility only if we can gather all of the manuscripts together, including the originals. By doing this, we now can know for certainty that we have the Word of God. While those of this persuasion still believe in the inspiration of Scriptures as a fundamental of the faith, they are weak in their view of preservation. Perhaps a way to summarize the non-KJV fundamentalist position would be something like this:

1. Only the original autographs were inspired.
2. Copies can be trusted to the extent that they conform to the originals.

3. We have no originals.
4. God has not promised to preserve His Word.
5. The Word of God is not found exclusively in any one translation, manuscript, or family of manuscripts.
6. We can observe from history that God has preserved His Word through the 5,600+ extant manuscripts.
7. We scholars will find it for you eventually.

It becomes apparent as one reads through the different quotes by well-meaning, conservative evangelical scholarship that there is much disagreement as a result of fallible human intellect. The position of these scholars will *never* give us a perfect or certain Bible. More important than the position of the scholars is the position of the Scriptures. What does the Bible say in reference to preservation? What is the biblical truth that can settle the questions that are constantly being asked today? Does the Bible teach its own preservation or does it not?

Preservation is implicit in the trust that biblical writers had in the Scripture. This can be proven by demonstrating what people in the Bible thought of their Scriptures. Jesus quoted the Old Testament in Matthew 21:42, Luke 4:21, and John 7:38. In John 5:39, Jesus commanded the Jews to *"Search the scriptures"*—these were not the original autographs; these were trusted, preserved copies.

When we read the story of the rich man and Lazarus in Luke 16, we find that Abraham recognized the trustworthiness of the Scriptures. When the rich man wanted Lazarus to go to his brothers' house, Abraham responded by saying that his brothers had *"Moses and the prophets...."* Obviously, these brothers did not have the original copies of the Pentateuch. These brothers had not acquired the original manuscript where Jeremiah had penned his prophecies. The Scriptures that were available in the rich man's days were trusted (preserved) copies.

When Paul writes his "last words" before meeting Jesus, he instructs Timothy in the power of the Scriptures. In 2 Timothy 3:15–16, we learn that Timothy had heard the Scriptures *"from a child...."* Again, Paul was completely confident in the Scriptures (i.e., copies of copies of copies) that were available.

The disciples believed that they had something more sure than oral prophecies. In 2 Peter 1:21 and John 19:24, 36–37, we find their position on the Scriptures. Paul told Timothy to study the Word of God (2 Timothy 2:15) as well as to preach the Word of God (2 Timothy 4:1–2). These commands are nonsensical unless there is an implied promise of the preservation of Scriptures.

Finally, notice how often Paul appeals to the Scriptures as he argues for righteous living and trusting Christ completely. The Scriptures were viewed as his final authority. In Romans 4:3, he states, *"...what saith the scripture?"* You can also see this philosophy demonstrated in Romans 9–11 where he constantly quotes the Old Testament to bolster his argument for the Jews to trust Christ (see specifically Romans 9:17 and 10:11). In Galatians 4:30 and 1 Timothy 5:18, he alludes to the Scriptures as authoritative as well. Did Paul have any of these original Old Testament Scriptures? No. He only had copies—yet copies that were completely trustworthy and recognized as authoritative Scriptures.

Here is what we observe from studying the believer's position on the Scriptures. None of these people, our Lord Jesus Christ included, ever corrected the Word of God. They simply quoted it.

The Scriptures, therefore teach us that preservation is implicit in the trust of Scripture. However, there is more. The Scriptures also show us that preservation is explicit in the teaching of Scriptures.

First, God promises that He will preserve His Word. In Psalm 119:152, we read: *"Concerning thy testimonies, I have known of old that thou hast founded them for ever."* How long must the Bible last for this promise to be true? Forever!

Second, Isaiah 59:21 states: *"As for me, this is my covenant with them, saith the LORD; My Spirit that is upon thee, and my words which I have put in thy mouth, shall not depart out of thy mouth, nor* out of the mouth of thy seed, nor out of the mouth of thy seed's seed, saith the LORD, from henceforth and for ever." The words start with God. He puts it into Isaiah's mouth, and the words are continually passed on forever.

Again, John 10:35 states that the "...scripture cannot be broken." If God gave His Word and part of it is now missing, the Scriptures are now broken. Who is right—God or man?

In conclusion, in Acts 7:38 we read, "This is he, that was in the church in the wilderness with the angel which spake to him in the mount Sina, and with our fathers: who received the lively oracles to give unto us." Our fathers received them and gave them to us. Even with copies we still have the "lively oracles."

These are just a few samples of where the Bible gives us explicit statements about the preservation of Scriptures. For further reference, see these verses:

> "The counsel of the LORD standeth for ever, the thoughts of his heart to all generations."—PSALM 33:11

> "For the LORD is good; his mercy is everlasting; and his truth endureth to all generations."—PSALM 100:5

> "Blessed are they that keep his testimonies, and that seek him with the whole heart."—PSALM 119:2

> "I will praise thee with uprightness of heart, when I shall have learned thy righteous judgments. I will keep thy statutes: O forsake me not utterly."—PSALM 119:7–8

> "For ever, O LORD, thy word is settled in heaven. Thy faithfulness is unto all generations: thou hast established the earth, and it abideth."—PSALM 119:89–90

> "Heaven and earth shall pass away, but my words shall not pass away."—MATTHEW 24:35

"Heaven and earth shall pass away: but my words shall not pass away."—LUKE 21:33

It is clear that God has promised to preserve His Word. Yet, He has also prompted us to perform His Word. Psalm 119:9 says, *"Wherewithal shall a young man cleanse his way? by taking heed thereto according to thy word."* This command is impossible if the Word of God is not preserved.

Study the commands and promises of these verses: Psalm 119:16, 22, 42, 60, 69, 93, and Proverbs 22:20–21. How can these verses be true unless the words of Scripture are preserved? God preserves His Words not so that we can argue over which text is correct; rather, He has preserved His Word so that we can spread it to every creature.

Those who advocate the Westcott and Hort position (i.e., the Critical Text) always have trouble with the preservation issue because it negates their practice. In the question of Bible translations, one either has a "preserved" Bible or a "restored, reconstructed" Bible.

Chapter Five In Summary

1. There are four primary positions on the Word of God.

2. The liberal position is characterized by "unbelief" and views the Bible as allegorical literature not to be interpreted literally and not to be given authority in belief or practice.

3. The neo-orthodox position is characterized by "unbelief disguised" and generally redefines Bible terms to fit a different belief system.

4. The new evangelical position is characterized as "belief compromised" because this position seeks to fellowship with the neo-orthodox and liberal positions.

5. The fundamental position is characterized by "belief" and seeks to believe the Bible literally and to make it the final authority in all matters of faith and practice.

6. Historically, biblical fundamentalists have stood for the following doctrines: the inerrancy of Scripture, the virgin birth and deity of Christ, the vicarious atonement of Christ, the bodily resurrection of Christ, and the visible return of Christ.

7. There are many who believe fundamental Bible doctrines who do not believe in using only the King James Version of the Bible.

8. The Bible issues boil down to a basic thought: we either have a "preserved Word," or we have a "being restored Word."

Understanding the Text—Part 1

Whenever one determines to study the translation issue, he will inevitably be led to research the textual issue. According to Peter's statement of faith given under the inspiration of the Holy Spirit, it is possible to have something that is certain—"a more sure word of prophecy."

Whereas Peter spoke of something more sure, today's believer is constantly bombarded with a newer and better translation that does not generate more trust. Rather, it generates confusion, doubt, dissension, and unending debate.

The textual issue can be summarized in three statements: 1) There is a *conflict* which involves primarily two texts (or two cities: Antioch and Alexandria). 2) The *character* of the men behind these texts should at least be evaluated. 3) There are some important *considerations* to be made in order to make an informed decision of faith and trust.

The Conflict

As noted, while there may be hundreds of *translations* on the market, there are—for all practical purposes—only two *texts*. Terms mentioned in this debate may often be misunderstood. For example, one often hears about manuscript evidence, about the texts of the early churches, and about translations used by **the fathers**. What does all of this mean? A manuscript is a partial (though theoretically it could be complete) copy of Scripture. It may contain a chapter, a book, or just a few verses. A text is either an attempt by men or the providential move of God to take all of the partial manuscripts and compile them into one source for the reader. A translation is an attempt by man (hopefully, but not always, under the guidance of God) to render this text into the common vernacular of the people with whom he is working.

With these terms being understood, we come again to the conflict of two competing texts in Christendom. One text is known as the Critical Text, the Minority Text, the "Eclectic" Text, the Westcott-Hort Text, the Egyptian Text, the Alexandrian Text, the Nestle-Aland Text or the United Bible Societies Text. The last two are so similar that sometimes critics will use the symbol "NU" referring

---

NOTABLE NAMES

The Fathers: Refers to the writings of the preachers, missionaries, scholars, etc., who quoted from the Scriptures. Where their writings quote the Scriptures, they verify the Greek text as it was written in the second century onward. Anti-Nicene fathers are of particular importance since their quotes would be of a text prior to AD 325.

Theodore Beza: He was the successor of John Calvin at Geneva. He also continued the line of Received Text editions. His 1598 Greek edition was also used heavily by the King James translators. Beza believed his manuscripts were influenced by Waldensian Christians—an early group of Christians, outside of Catholicism, dating back to AD 120.

---

to these two texts as the Nestle and UBS combined. Each of these names carries a slightly different nuance with it, but substantially each of these terms represents the same body of a corrupt stream of texts. Don't let the multiplicity of terms confuse you.

The second grouping of similar texts is known as the Received Text, the Preserved Text, the Textus Receptus, the TR, the Traditional Text, the Majority Text, the Byzantine Text, the Antiochian Text, or the Syrian Text. Again, each name carries a different connotation but all essentially refer to the same body of proven, God-preserved texts—we'll revisit this in a later chapter.

The term *Received Text* or *Preserved Text* implies that this text was received from Christ (the Head) via the apostles by the local churches and preserved by God. The term *Traditional Text* implies that this text has been traditionally used by the churches from the time of Christ through this present time. The term *Byzantine Text* implies that the Greek-speaking Christians of the Byzantine empire recognized that this Greek text was superior to anything coming from Alexandria. (The autographs of Scripture were sent toward the Byzantine Empire; no autograph was sent to Alexandria. This gives the Byzantine text a "head start" in establishing itself as the correct text validated and used by the early churches.)

The term *Antiochian Text* draws attention to the fact that Christians were first called Christians in Antioch (of Syria, hence the Syrian Text). This city was also the place from which missionaries were first sent (Acts 13). There is also the possibility that the church in this city translated the Greek text into the Syriac Peshitta as well as the Old Latin Itala.

Interestingly, these Itala Christians would later come to be known as the Waldenses or Vaudois (people of the valleys). These Christians were recognized by **Beza** as the remainder of the most pure primitive Christian church. Jean Leger, a Waldensian pastor and leader during the seventeenth century stated that they have "always had the entire joy and fruition of the celestial treasure of the true preserved holy Scriptures."[1] History records that the Catholic church attempted to remove this "sect" from the earth, destroying many of their Bibles.

While those who embrace the Critical Text may not totally agree with the philosophy or methodology of Westcott and Hort, the term *Westcott-Hort Text* simply implies that these men were two of the early influencers in leading churches away from the Received Text in the late 1800s. There are orthodox men who feel the Critical Text is superior to the Received Text. These men would not associate with the unorthodoxy of Westcott and Hort.

Nevertheless, if we are to understand the Critical Text, we must take into consideration that it had its beginnings with two men who were at worst, unbelievers, and at best representative of the liberal side of Christendom. We will document this further in the next chapter.

While these men referred to 45 out of 5,255 manuscripts, their new Greek text was overwhelmingly based on two manuscripts— Aleph and B (B predominantly). These manuscripts disagree in 5,604 places. The Critical Text and the Received Text disagree about 7–10% of the time.[2]

This new text produced by Westcott and Hort relied heavily on two manuscripts: the Vaticanus (sometimes called "B") and the Sinaiticus (sometimes called "Aleph"). In essence, these two manuscripts were to revolutionize the way Christianity viewed

---

DEFINING THE TERMS

Vellum: *A term for a manuscript written on expensive calfskin. This was far more superior than the ancient papyri.*

Uncials: *A manuscript that is written in large, capital letters. Also called a "Majuscule."*

---

the Bible. The Vaticanus was not available for open scholarship until 1889.

> Vaticanus is said to be the oldest extant (existing) **vellum** manuscript. It and the Codex Sinaiticus are the two oldest **uncial** manuscripts. They were probably written in the fourth century. The Vaticanus was placed in the Vatican Library at Rome by Pope Nicolas V in 1448, its previous history being unknown. Most likely it originally consisted of a complete copy of the Septuagint and of the New Testament. It is now imperfect, and consists of 759 thin, delicate leaves, of which the New Testament fills 142. Like the Sinaiticus, it is primarily of value to critical biblical scholars in aiding in the formation of a "correct text" of the New Testament. It is referred to by critics as Codex B.[3]

Even though 95–99% of all manuscripts favored the Received Text, all of this evidence was to be overturned on the basis of a manuscript found and housed in the Vatican and a manuscript found in a Greek monastery at Mount Sinai by **Constantin Von Tischendorf**, a man who had given his life to "restore" the text of the early church. Tischendorf describes his philosophy best:

> I resolved, in 1839, to devote myself to the textual study of the New Testament, and attempted, by making use of all the acquisitions of the last three centuries, to reconstruct, if possible, the exact text, as it came from the

---

NOTABLE NAMES

Constantin Von Tischendorf: A German textual critic who lived his life with the quest of restoring the true biblical text. He is credited with finding Codex Sinaiticus at St. Catherine's Greek Monastery at Mount Sinai. He believed the Textus Receptus (Received Text) did not match the original writings and set out to reconstruct the "pure text."

---

pen of the sacred writers. My first critical edition of the New Testament appeared in the autumn of 1840. But after giving this edition a final revision, I came to the conviction that to make use even of our existing materials would call for a more attentive study than they had hitherto received, and I resolved to give my leisure and abilities to a fresh examination of the original documents...Learned men have again and again attempted to clear the sacred text from these extraneous elements. But we have at last hit upon a better plan even than this, which is to set aside this Textus Receptus altogether, and to construct a fresh text, derived immediately from the most ancient and authoritative sources. This is undoubtedly the right course to take, for in this way only can we secure a text approximating as closely as possible to that which came from the apostles....[4]

Tischendorf began his journey with the purpose of reconstructing the exact text of Scripture. In other words, his preconceived idea was that the Received Text was corrupt in places and needed to be amended to reflect the original autographs (which no longer existed). He was working from the very beginning with the faulty supposition that God's supernatural preservation work had not occurred. He was presuming that all present texts were corrupt. In other words, he had a predetermined bias that the Word of God needed to be corrected. He was determined to expose the fault that he was already sure of and then to fix it.

With this "faith" in restoring God's Word, he searched near and far for ancient manuscripts. In 1844, at St. Catherines' Monastery at Mount Sinai, he found what would be known as Sinaiticus. The librarian told him that these pages were consigned to the fire as rubbish. To say it another way, this *Greek* Orthodox monastery saw no value in the *Greek* manuscripts that Tischendorf "found." It was these rejected pages that formed, along with Vaticanus (whose history is unknown), the primary basis for the Critical Text.

As Westcott and Hort began their work, it is important to understand that they were *not* commissioned to create either a new Greek text or a new "version" or translation.

These instructions were given to Westcott and Hort along with their Revision Committee:

> 1) That it is desirable that a revision of the Authorized Version of the Holy Scriptures be undertaken. 2) That the revision be so conducted as to comprise both marginal renderings and such emendations as it may be found necessary to insert in the text of the Authorized Version. 3) That in the above resolutions we *do not contemplate any new translation of the Bible.* [emphasis added], or any alteration of the language, except where, in the judgment of the most competent scholars, such change is necessary.[5]

Bishop Ellicott, who was the Chairman of the Committee, made this observation: "Nothing is more satisfactory at the present time than the evident feelings of veneration for our Authorized Version, and *the very generally-felt desire for as little change as possible* [emphasis added]."[6]

Again, Ellicott stated that, "…our object was to revise a version, not to frame a text."[7]

Westcott and Hort were not commissioned to create a new text, and they were far from transparent and open about their work. Alfred Martin noted, "Westcott and Hort had been working on their text since 1853; in 1870 they printed a tentative edition for private distribution only. This they circulated under pledge of *secrecy* within the company of New Testament revisers, of which they were members. It soon became evident that the New Testament committee was not going to be content merely to revise the Authorized Version, but was determined to revise the underlying Greek text radically."[8]

As a result of Westcott and Hort's philosophy, as well as their bias against the Received Text, they produced a shorter (less complete) text. Each believed that the shorter reading was to be preferred. Why? Perhaps it can be explained by the fact that Hort gave evidence that he leaned toward Darwin's theory of evolution.

"It certainly startles me to find you saying that you have seen no facts which support such view as Darwin's. But I do see immense difficulties in his theory, some of which might by this time have been removed, if he had understood more clearly the conditions of his problem. But it seems to me the most probable manner of development, and the reflexions suggested by his book drove me to the conclusion that some kind of development must be supposed."[9]

This paradigm can also be seen in their view of textual criticism. In their minds, the Received Text (which is longer) evolved over time as scribes made "emendations" or "conflated" (or harmonized) two similar passages.

With an understanding of how the Westcott-Hort Text developed, we see a completely different picture when studying the Received Text. This text is longer than its counterpart. Advocates of the Critical Text point out that the Received Text has evolved over the years. Proponents of the Received Text point to the removal of key Christological passages from the Critical Text, causing it to be a shorter text. The fact is undeniable: one text is longer; one text is shorter. How those facts are interpreted by each position is the crux of the debate.

The Received Text is based on 5,210 out of 5,255 manuscripts according to Waite (remember the Critical Text uses 45 manuscripts). Interestingly, even Westcott and Hort recognized the Received Text as being universally accepted and used by the churches from about 450–1850 AD. Some would even allow for this text to be dominant in the fourth century (350 AD). Notice Alfred Martin's observations: "…it embodies substantially the text which even Westcott and Hort admit was dominant in the church from the middle of the fourth century on. The text used by the Church Fathers from

Chrysostom's time on was not materially different from the text of Erasmus and Stephanus."[10]

Since the church is the pillar and ground of the truth according to 1 Timothy 3:15, it is important to notice what this institution has accepted as the "Word of God" from its inception. History bears record that the Traditional Text has been used by local Bible-believing churches since the book of Acts.

The Character of the Critical Text

The credibility of a witness is determined by the character of that witness. If Westcott and Hort were to be on trial along with the manuscripts that support their Revised Greek Text, would their verdict be guilty for falsifying the Scriptures?

Dr. F.H.A. Scrivener, a man associated with Westcott and Hort's Revision Committee made the following observation about the manuscripts on which it heavily relied: "[The Codex Sinaiticus]

NOTABLE NAMES

Chrysostom: John Chrysostom (354–407) was born in Antioch, Syria. He was born into a wealthy family but later went into a monastic life. In 386, he began preaching, earning the nickname, Chrysostom, which means "golden-mouth." After making a reference to the Empress in his sermon, he was exiled. He died during a forced march and was considered a martyr by the Syrian church.

Erasmus: His contribution to the textual issue is the Greek Text he edited and printed in 1516, followed by four other editions. He led the way in going back to a Greek source, rather than a Latin source for the Bible. (See expanded definition, p. 191.)

Robert Stephanus: Also known as Robert Stephens and Estienne. He continued the line of Received Text editions. His 1550 Greek edition was a major contributor to the King James translators. Incidentally, he was also the one to give us verse divisions.

---

is covered with such alterations, brought in by *at least* ten different revisers, some of them systematically spread over every page… [emphasis his]."[11]

He noticed ten different handwriting styles in the one manuscript. Why was there a need for ten different people to continue correcting this manuscript? Because those who first handled it felt it was not a good manuscript! You do not cross words out because you think they are right; you cross them out in order to correct them.

Are you connecting the dots? The Critical Text was assembled under the guise of revision, and it was based on two manuscripts that heavily disagree between themselves and that literally contain crossed-out words, omissions, and the handwriting of several different scribes. Why would scholars attach mountains of value to these manuscripts merely because they are presumed to be old? Modern-day scholars actually *prefer* the disagreement of the Critical Text over the consistency of the Received Text!

Dabney, in his work on the Greek New Testament, observed this about the character of Westcott and Hort's underlying manuscripts:

> …the Vatican, the Alexandrian, and now the Sinai. *It is expressly admitted that neither of these has an extant*

NOTABLE NAMES

F.H.A. Scrivener: *This man lived from 1813–1891. He was a British writer and manuscript editor, and a contemporary of scholars such as Westcott and Hort. He did not share their views. After serving on the Revision Committee with Westcott and Hort, he distanced himself from that project by editing his own edition of the Received Text in 1881.*

Dean John William Burgon: *(1813–1888) He was an Anglican minister and "Dean of Chichester"—a staunch defender of the Traditional Text and of the "faith once delivered." He strongly opposed the methodology and theories of Westcott and Hort and the revised Greek texts.*

history. No documentary external evidence exists as to the names of the copyists who transcribed them, the date, or the place of their writing. *Nobody knows whence the Vatican MS came to the Pope's library, or how long it has been there...Tischendorf himself was unable to trace the presence of his favorite Codex, in the monastery of St. Catherine on Mt. Horeb, by external witnesses, higher than the twelfth century. Their early date is confessedly assigned by conjecture* [in other words—"we guessed!"]... [emphasis added].[12]

What Dabney points out is that when a scholar states that this reading is based on "older manuscripts" as a fact, it is in reality a statement of faith—scholarly guesswork!

John William Burgon, a strong proponent of the Traditional Text and outspoken critic of Westcott and Hort stated, "...the scribe, whose plan is...to begin every fresh book of the Bible at the top of the next ensuing column to that which contained the concluding words of the preceding book, has at the close of St. Mark's Gospel deviated from his else invariable practice. *He has left in this place one column entirely vacant. It is the only vacant column in the whole manuscript—a blank space abundantly sufficient to contain the twelve verses which he nevertheless withheld* [emphasis added]."[13] Out of 620 Greek manuscripts that contain the Gospel of Mark, only two omit the last twelve verses—Vaticanus and Sinaiticus, and both of these actually have blank space where the verses belong!

In other words, it appears as though the scribes—for reasons unknown—left out the concluding verses to the Gospel of Mark,

DEFINING THE TERMS

Lectionaries: These are not biblical manuscripts, per se, but were collections of Scripture lessons arranged for congregational readings. They would "contain" Scripture.

yet he was aware that they belonged there, thus leaving ample space for their inclusion. In regards to the end of Mark 16, these twelve verses are found to be used by the early church in their **lectionaries** (a book or listing that contains a collection of Scripture readings for worship—usually cyclical in nature), thus showing the universal acceptance of these verses as authentic *before* the supposed dates of the Sinaiticus manuscript. This passage is also verified by the afore mentioned second century Bibles—Syriac Peshitta and The Old Latin.

Burgon stated in one of his other works:

> [I am] utterly disinclined to believe—so grossly improbable does it seem—that at the end of 1,800 years 995 copies out of every thousand, suppose will prove untrustworthy; and that the one, two, three, four, or five which remain, whose contents till yesterday as good as unknown, will be found to have retained the secret of what the Holy Spirit originally inspired. I am utterly unable to believe, in short, that God's promise has so entirely failed, that at the end of 1800 years much of the text of the Gospel has in point of fact to be picked by a German critic out of a waste paper basket in the convent of St. Catherine; and that the entire text had to be remodelled after the pattern set by a couple of copies which had remained in neglect during fifteen centuries, and had probably owed their survival to that neglect; whilst hundreds of others had been thumbed to pieces, and had bequeathed their witness to copies made from them.[14]

There is more evidence to the character of the Critical Text that must be noted. For example, Thomas Strouse observed that the Critical Text has a historical error in Matthew 1:7, 10. In the Received Text, two kings are in Christ's lineage—namely, Asa and Amon. Metzger, in advocating for the Critical Text, believed that Matthew may have received his information from faulty genealogical records, thus the Critical Text substitutes the names Asaph and Amos into the lineage.

Second, there is a scientific error in Luke 23:45. The Critical Text uses a Greek word meaning "was eclipsed" whereas the Received Text uses a word meaning "was darkened." It would have been a scientific impossibility for the sun to have been eclipsed during the season of Passover because the moon was full.

Third, as we saw previously, there is a Christ-contradicting error found in John 7:8. In the Critical Text, Christ states that He will not go up to the Feast, and then He goes. These types of errors demonstrate the character of the Critical Text and the view of its editors regarding inerrancy of Scripture.[15]

The evidence concerning the character of the Critical Text and its underlying manuscripts raises several questions:

1. Why did the early church not embrace the readings of Alexandria, Egypt?

2. Why can no documented history be found concerning the origins of this different text?

3. If scholarship believes the dates assigned to these "older" manuscripts are based on conjecture and cannot be documented past the twelfth century, why does scholarship continually state that these are older manuscripts—as though this was a substantiated fact?

4. How could the church be wrong for fifteen centuries, only to have the correct text restored based upon a few manuscripts with a shady history?

5. Why would God's inspired words contradict themselves and not be truthfully accurate?

The fact that we find inconsistencies within the Critical Text theory, does not make the Received Text accurate by default. We must be willing to examine the character of the Received Text just as thoroughly as that of the Critical Text. Ellicott, a member of

Westcott and Hort's Revision Committee, had this to say about the Received Text: "The manuscripts which Erasmus used differ, for the most part, only in small and insignificant details from the bulk of the cursive manuscripts. The general character of their text is the same. *By this observation the pedigree of the Received Text is carried up beyond the individual manuscripts used by Erasmus...That pedigree stretches back to a remote antiquity. The first ancestor of the Received Text was at least contemporary with the oldest of our extant manuscripts, if not older than any one of them* [emphasis added]."[16]

Burgon, the defender of the Traditional Text *par excellence* stated, "Strange as it may appear, it is undeniably true, that the whole of the controversy may be reduced to the following narrow issue: Does the truth of the text of Scripture dwell with the vast multitude of copies, uncial and cursive, concerning which nothing is more remarkable than the marvelous agreement which subsists between them? Or is it rather to be supposed that the truth abides exclusively with a very little handful of manuscripts, which at once differ from the great bulk of the witnesses, and—strange to say— also amongst themselves?"[17]

Burgon also writes, "Call this Text Erasmian or Complutensian— the Text of Stephens, or of Beza or of the Elzevirs—call it the 'Received' or the 'Traditional Greek Text,' or whatever other name you please—the fact remains, that a text has come down to us which is attested by a general consensus of ancient copies, ancient versions, and ancient fathers."[18]

CHAPTER SIX IN SUMMARY

1. Practically speaking, there are only two Bible texts from which all English Bible versions are sourced. The Received Text can be traced to the historical record of the true church, and the Critical Text is traced to a relatively few obscure manuscripts.

2. The Critical Text introduced changes based upon 45 out of 5,255 manuscripts. These 45 texts disagree amongst themselves in over 5,600 places, but because of their age were deemed to be more "accurate."

3. The two most prominent ancient manuscripts are Vaticanus and Sinaiticus. These texts were found in the 1800s and presumed to date back to the fourth century. They disagree with themselves over 3,000 times in the Gospels alone and both show clear signs of corruption.

4. Constantin Von Tischendorf, the man who found Sinaiticus, had a preconceived bias against the Received Text and created a text with thousands of changes based upon one manuscript.

5. Westcott and Hort privately introduced and later published a new Greek text in the late 1800s that was based upon the earlier work of Tischendorf.

6. The character of the Critical Text is flawed and the logic behind it reaches many illogical conclusions.

Understanding the Text—Part 2

As we consider the texts that are used for the translation of the Bible, it is important to consider the beliefs and perspective of those involved in the process of preparing the text. Are we being handed God's Word from a group of men that respect that word and generally believe it to be "from God"? Or are we being given the Word of God by men who view it merely as a work of literature with no eternal significance? In the coming pages, we will see what these men said for themselves.

Considering the Critical Text

Imagine you are a missionary attempting to translate the Bible into a language that does not have God's Word. What do you need to know about how to choose the correct text?

It is appropriate to understand what formed the philosophy for Westcott and Hort's undertaking to give the world a new Greek text.

First, Hort did not believe the Scriptures to be infallible.
Here are his own words about this subject:

> If you make a decided conviction of the absolute
> infallibility of the New Testament practically a sine qua
> non [an essential] for cooperation, I fear I could not
> join you, even if you were willing to forget your fears
> about the origin of the Gospels. I am most anxious to
> find the New Testament infallible, and have a strong
> sense of the Divine purpose guiding all its parts; but I
> cannot see how the exact limits of such guidance can be
> ascertained...I suppose, you would say that any apparent
> errors discovered by criticism are only apparent, and
> that owing to the imperfection of our knowledge. I fully
> believe that this is true of a large proportion of what the
> rasher critics peremptorily pronounce to be errors; and
> I think it *possible* that it may be true of all, but as far as
> my present knowledge goes, hardly *probable*.[1]

**Second, Hort firmly believed that no one ever attempted
to change Scripture in order to promote false doctrine.** Wilbur
Pickering quotes Hort as saying, "There are no signs of deliberate
falsification of the text for dogmatic purposes."[2]

Hort's belief, however, contradicts Scripture. The Scriptures
record that even while the apostles were still alive there were those
who were corrupting and changing the Scriptures. Peter mentions
those who "wrest" the Scriptures, referring to Paul's epistles
(2 Peter 3:15–16). Paul referred to the "many" who corrupted the
Word of God (2 Corinthians 2:17) and the possibility of handling
the Word of God deceitfully (2 Corinthians 4:2).

Hort's belief also contradicts history. **Polycarp**, a disciple of
the Apostle John, stated that "Whoever perverts the saying...of the
Lord, that one is the firstborn of Satan." Tatian, a "Christian" living
from 110–172, wrote the Diatessaron, which was a combination of
the four Gospel narratives into one. This work was so corrupted
that in later years a bishop of Syria threw out two hundred copies

since church members were mistaking it for the true Gospel. Gaius, an Orthodox Father who wrote between 175–200 AD, named Asclepiades, Theodotus, Hermophilus, and Apolomides as heretics who prepared corrupted copies of the Scriptures and had disciples who multiplied these copies.

Origen stated in reference to the tampering of manuscripts in his day, "Nowadays, as is evident, there is a great diversity between the various manuscripts, either through the negligence of certain copyists, or the perverse audacity shown by some in correcting the text, or through the fault of those, who, playing the part of correctors, lengthen or shorten it as they please."[3] Notice how both Scripture and history contradict the statement by Hort.

Third, Westcott and Hort believed that the Traditional Text (which contained the majority of manuscript agreement) could be explained by a collective effort of the church. This led them to the idea of "weighing" the manuscripts rather than "counting" them. Terrance Brown explains, "Their theory was that there must have been some kind of deliberate but misguided editorial revision of the Greek Text, probably in Syria, possibly in Antioch, perhaps during the latter part of the fourth century…. According to this theory, this edited text was wrongly permitted to eclipse the 'pure' text exhibited by B and Aleph—until these documents were rehabilitated in the nineteenth century."[4]

NOTABLE NAMES

Polycarp: An early Christian leader who pastored the church at Smyrna. As a disciple of John, he had first hand knowledge about apostolic writings. His letters agree with the Traditional Text.

Origen: Lived from AD 185–254. He followed Clement as head of the "Christian" school at Alexandria which was a blend of Gnosticism and Christianity. He was a pioneer in textual criticism and believed in an allegorical interpretation of Scripture—using symbolism rather than literal meanings of words.

Burgon stated the following in his work *Revision Revised:*

> Somewhere between AD 250 and 350, therefore, ("it
> is impossible to say with confidence" [here, Burgon is
> quoting Hort sarcastically] what was the actual date, but
> these editors evidently incline to the latter half of the
> third century, i.e., circa AD 275) we are to believe that
> the ecclesiastical heads of the four great patriarchates of
> Eastern Christendom—Alexandria, Antioch, Jerusalem,
> and Constantinople—had become so troubled at
> witnessing the prevalence of depraved copies of Holy
> Scripture in their respective churches that they resolved,
> by common consent, to achieve an authoritative revision
> which should henceforth become the standard text of all
> the patriarchates of the East.[5]

This is the conflation theory that we discussed earlier (also
called the "Lucian Recension" and the "Syrian Recension") and it is
another belief based solely on conjecture (i.e., this is how it could
have happened…) rather than evidence. It is scholarly "spin" when,
in fact, all the evidence points the other way!

**Fourth, Westcott and Hort believed in a Syrian Recension
where these church leaders met and established what would
become the basis for the Byzantine or Received Text.** They never
give any evidence, never quote any church fathers who were involved,
etc. In other words, it is as though they have invented history solely
from their own preconceived ideas. There is no historical evidence
for this alleged event in church history.

**Fifth, Westcott and Hort believed that the older manuscripts
were more likely to be better.** Glenny makes this statement, speaking
against the Received Text, "The fact that no Greek manuscript with
this text-type is known from before the fourth century makes it
questionable if it existed before that time."[6]

Yet, this quote could just as easily be turned against the
Critical Text. As noted earlier, Ellicott stated that the first ancestor

of the Received Text was at least contemporary with the oldest of our extant manuscripts, if not older than any one of them. Again, we noticed earlier that Dabney stated that the early date for the Critical Text is assigned by conjecture. The inference being that "if no Greek manuscript with this text-type [i.e., the Critical Text] is known from before the fourth century makes it questionable if it existed before that time." In other words, a blanket statement about "oldest being best" is arbitrary at best.

Sixth, Westcott and Hort also believed that the shorter reading is more likely to be accurate than the longer reading. "In the New Testament, as in almost all prose writings which have been much copied, corruptions by interpolation are many times more numerous than corruptions by omission."[7]

Finally, these two believed there were many errors and mistakes made by the scribes. "For over 1,400 years the New Testament was copied by hand, and the copyists (scribes) made every conceivable error, as well as at times intentionally altering (probably with the idea of 'correcting') the text."[8] This low view of the men involved does not allow for a high view of providential or miraculous preservation. This view inevitably leads to men restoring Scripture rather than God preserving it for each generation.

This view also presumes that those copying Scripture through the ages did not revere or value it—a supposition that tells us more about the character of Westcott and Hort than the character of early Christian scribes.

As you consider which text reflects the more accurate reading, it helps to know the history associated with it. The Critical Text originated with men who did not believe the Scriptures to be infallible. They were men willing to re-write history by promoting the notion that no one ever deliberately changed Scriptures for doctrinal purposes and they taught a theory as fact concerning the alleged Syrian Recension. These men held that the majority of manuscripts agreed together due to a collective effort of the church to "inflate" the doctrines of Christ. They claim that, while noble in its attempt, this effort had a negative effect on the text of Scripture (a text which they have restored). (A similar argument was presented in Dan Brown's fictional novel *The Da Vinci Code*.)

These men, led by Westcott and Hort, were willing to throw away 5,210 manuscripts for two that they "conjectured" were older. Again, they held that men were more apt to add to Scripture rather than take away, hence the shorter reading was to be preferred. They did not believe God could preserve His Word but that scribes made every mistake imaginable. Men on their own committee such as Scrivener and Ellicott saw the superiority of the Greek Textus Receptus and questioned Hort's true intentions. Scrivener, after the revision, edited his own Textus Receptus, choosing to have his name associated with what the churches recognized through the centuries rather than the apostasy associated with the new text.

There is much to consider about the Critical Text that was begun by Westcott and Hort and continued today by Nestle and Aland. There are also considerations to be made about the Received Text. If one were to choose the Received Text, what must he understand?

Considering the Received Text

Those who have held to the superiority of the Textus Receptus (and its subsequent translations such as the Tyndale, Geneva, Bishops, Coverdale, and King James Bibles) have believed the Scriptures to be infallible. Notice this quote from someone who was not a friend to the Received Text: "...Burgon believed in the inerrancy of Scripture and Hort et al. did not...."[9]

Those holding to a Received Text view teach that there were false teachers who attempted to corrupt the Word of God. Origen, an influential leader from the church at Alexandria during the second and third centuries, "...taught that the soul existed from eternity before it inhabited the body, and that after death, it migrated to a higher or a lower form of life according to the deeds done in the body; and finally all would return to the state of pure intelligence, only to begin again the same cycles as before. He believed that the devils would be saved, and that the stars and planets had souls, and were, like men, on trial to learn perfection."[10]

Origen also believed that the "Scriptures are of little use to those who understand them as they are written."[11] Origen advocated an **allegorical** approach to Scripture and saw no merit in the **literal** hermeneutical approach taught in Antioch by true Christians.

F.H.A. Scrivener states: "It is no less true to fact than paradoxical in sound, that the worst corruptions, to which the New Testament has ever been subjected, originated within a hundred years after it was composed; that Irenaeus [AD 150] and the African Fathers, and the whole Western, with a portion of the Syrian Church, used far inferior manuscripts to those employed by Stunica, or Erasmus, or Stephens thirteen centuries later, when molding the Textus Receptus."[12]

Furthermore, those who believe that God has preserved His Word through Bible-believing churches via the Received Text find no evidence for any alleged "Syrian Recension."

DEFINING THE TERMS

Allegorical Interpretation: An interpretative process that stems from the searching of hidden meanings in the text. The literal words are not as important as the hidden or esoterical meaning to be found. This interpretative model does not emphasize the words, but rather the hidden concepts.

Literal Interpretation: An interpretative process that stems from the study of the exact words used in their context. What do these words mean? The emphasis is on the words that were deliberately chosen by the Holy Spirit.

"The weakness of Westcott and Hort's theory of a fourth century Syrian revision which resulted in the substitution of the majority text for the B/Aleph text is that such a revision is unknown to history. The whole scheme rests upon a supposition for which there is no historical evidence, and consists largely in making dogmatic assertions based upon uncertainties."[13]

While Westcott and Hort believed that "oldest was best," those who hold to a Received Text position believe that the two manuscripts so trusted and cherished by Westcott and Hort were particularly unreliable.

The clarity of Burgon's thoughts are powerful concerning this issue. "Who will venture to deny that those codices are indebted for their preservation solely to the circumstance, that they were long since recognized as the depositories of readings which rendered them utterly untrustworthy?"[14]

Those who hold to a Received Text position also see the longer text as being more accurate whereas the shorter reading would be more prone to error. One author gives an insightful perspective here:

> The whole question of interpolations in ancient manuscripts has been set in an entirely new light by the researches of Mr. A.C. Clark, Corpus Professor of Latin at Oxford.... In the *Descent of Manuscripts*, an investigation of the manuscript tradition of the Greek and Latin Classics, he proves conclusively that the error to which scribes were most prone was not interpolation but accidental omission.... Hitherto the maxim *brevior lectio potior*...has been assumed as a postulate of scientific criticism. Clark has shown that, so far as classical texts are concerned, the facts point entirely the other way.[15]

Considering the Scribes Behind the Text

One final point to consider is which text shows the scribes' attention to detail. While the following information relates primarily to the

Old Testament, it does illustrate how the Jews viewed the Holy Scriptures. Considering that the first-century church was made largely of Jews in the beginning, it is hard to fathom that scribes made "every conceivable error." In fact, here is the way the Jews were taught to handle the Word of God:

1. The parchment must be made from the skin of clean animals; it must be prepared by a Jew only; and the skins must be fastened together by strings taken from clean animals.

2. Each column must have no less than 48 nor more than 60 lines. The entire copy must be first lined....

3. The ink must be of no other color than black, and it must be prepared according to a special recipe.

4. No word nor letter could be written from memory; the scribe must have an authentic copy before him, and he must read and pronounce aloud each word before writing it.

5. He must reverently wipe his pen each time before writing the word for "God," and he must wash his whole body before writing the name "Jehovah" lest the Holy Name be contaminated.

6. Strict rules were given concerning forms of the letters, spaces between letters, words, and sections, the use of the pen, the color of the parchment, etc.

7. The revision of a roll must be made within 30 days after the work was finished; otherwise it was worthless. One mistake on a sheet condemned the sheet; if three mistakes were found on any page, the entire manuscript was condemned.

8. Every word and every letter was counted, and if a letter was omitted, an extra letter inserted, or if one letter touched another, the manuscript was condemned and destroyed at once.[16]

Considering the Reliability of the Text

Still there is more that must be considered. One must consider the reliability of the text. When looking at the Westcott-Hort text, Warfield made an amazing statement. In effect, he called the eclectic text extremely corrupt and marvelously correct at the same time! Here is his statement in context:

> The best the press can do is measurably to stop the growth of corruption and faithfully to perpetuate all that has already grown. No wonder that the current New Testament text must be adjudged, in comparison with a well printed modern book, extremely corrupt.
>
> On the other hand, if we compare the present state of the New Testament text with that of any other ancient writing, we must render the opposite verdict, and declare it to be marvellously correct…such has been the providence of God in preserving for His Church in each and every age a competently exact text of the Scriptures….[17]

Warfield admitted that corruption was already present in his text, and that all one could do now was to stop its growth. Compare this to Burgon's statement about the Traditional Text:

> But my experience as one who has given a considerable amount of my attention to such subjects, tells me that the narrative before us carries on its front the impress of Divine origin. I venture to think that it vindicates for itself a high, unearthly meaning…the more I study it, the more I am pressed with its Divinity.

> I contend that on all intelligent principles of sound criticism the passage before us must be maintained to be genuine Scripture; and that without a particle of doubt.[18]

Here, it becomes clear as to which text is more reliable. One man, Warfield, holds his Critical Text in hand, determined to not let any more corruption in. Another man, Burgon, holds in his hand a text that is genuine Scripture without a trace of doubt. Peter thanked God for a *"more sure word...."* Which text best fits that description? The obvious answer to this question would be the Received Text.

We have considered some important reasons for choosing a text. We have noticed what others have said about the reliability of the text. What do we know about the research that went into the Critical Text?

The Critical Text has as its foundation mainly two manuscripts—namely Codex Aleph (from Mount Sinai) and Codex B (from the Vatican).

Tischendorf described his discovery as such:

> The desire which I felt to discover some precious remains of any manuscripts, more especially biblical, of a date which would carry us back to the early times of Christianity, was realized beyond my expectations. It was at the foot of Mount Sinai, in the Convent of St. Catherine, that I discovered the pearl of all my researches. In visiting the library of the monastery, in the month of May, 1844, I perceived in the middle of the great hall a large and wide basket full of old parchments; and the librarian, who was a man of information, told me that two heaps of papers like these, mouldered by time, had been already committed to the flames. What was my surprise to find amid this heap of papers a considerable number of sheets of a copy of the Old Testament in Greek, which seemed to me to be one of the most ancient that

I had ever seen. The authorities of the convent allowed me to possess myself of a third of these parchments, or about forty-three sheets, all the more readily as they were destined for the fire.[19]

It was another fifteen years before Tischendorf, under the patronage of the Czar of Russia, was allowed to retain possession of the whole Sinaitic Bible, including the New Testament, the Epistle of Barnabas, and the Shepherd of Hermas.

David Otis Fuller continues the account of Tischendorf along with a critical perspective given by Dean Burgon. "Naturally enough Dr. Tischendorf was highly elated by his discovery. Indeed his enthusiasm was unbounded. He says, 'I knew that I held in my hands the most precious biblical treasure in existence;' and he considered this discovery to be 'greater than that of the Koh-i-noor [diamond] of the Queen of England.'...We need not wonder, therefore, that the great scholar was carried away by his chance discovery, and that he succeeded in impressing upon others also his own idea of the surpassing importance of his 'find.'"

Dean Burgon aptly remarks: "Happy in having discovered [in 1859] an uncial Codex, second in antiquity only to the oldest before known [the Vatican Codex], and strongly resembling that famous fourth century Codex, he suffered his judgment to be overpowered by the circumstance. He at once remodeled his 7th edition [i.e., his 7th edition of the Greek text of the New Testament] in 3,505 places

---

Notable Names

Dr. Samuel Tregelles: British scholar and editor—1813–1875. Almost entirely self-taught, Tregelles was the British Tischendorf. He did not discover as many manuscripts, and he published only one edition of his Greek text; but he too spent much of his life gathering data; he and Tischendorf frequently compared collations. (See expanded definition, p. 194.)

---

to the scandal of the science of comparative criticism, as well as to his own grave discredit for discernment and consistency."[20]

Due solely to the antiquity of the age of this one single Codex, Tischendorf changed his previous text in 3,505 places. We are expected to believe that we almost lost God's Word as these monks in a Greek Monastery saw no merit for this Greek document and had consigned it to the fire.

The research behind the Vatican Manuscript is lacking as well. Dr. George Sayles Bishop states this about the research used to determine the validity of the Vaticanus:

> In 1845, **Dr. Samuel Tregelles**, armed with a letter from Cardinal Wiseman, went to Rome with the design of seeing the manuscript, Codex Vaticanus. After much trouble Dr. Tregelles did see it. "Two prelates were detailed to watch him, and they would not let him open the volume without previously searching his pockets and taking away from him ink and paper. Any prolonged study of a certain passage was the signal for snatching the book hurriedly away. He made some notes upon his cuffs and fingernails."
>
> In 1867 Tischendorf, by permission of Cardinal Antonelli, undertook to study this same Vatican Codex. He had nearly finished three Gospels when his efforts to transcribe them were discovered by a Prussian Jesuit spy. The book was immediately taken away. It was restored again, months later, by the intervention of Vercellone for a few hours. In all Tischendorf had the manuscript before him forty-two hours and only three hours at any one time, and all but a few of those hours were spent on the Gospels; and yet, he says, "I succeeded in preparing the whole New Testament for a new and reliable edition, so as to obtain every desired result."[21]

It is also important to note what kind of people are attracted to each text. The Critical Text is defended by a wide gamut of people.

There are orthodox and fundamental people who believe the Critical Text is better. I disagree with them, but still count them as brothers. The Critical Text is defended by heretics and unbelievers as well. Why is it that Jehovah's Witnesses, when "re-translating" their New World Translation, believed in the superiority of the Critical Text? Some would say the weakening of the deity of Christ as found in this text is more in line with their own teachings.

For instance, Dr. Paul Chappell shares a soulwinning story during which time he was sharing verses on the deity of Christ with a Jehovah's Witness man. After several moments of not being able to refute these verses, the man finally asked Dr. Chappell which version of the Bible he was using. When Dr. Chappell affirmed that he was using the King James version the man replied in angered frustration, "I hate that version!"

In contrast, when one sees who is championing the Received Text position, you find believers only. Why does the Received Text evoke that type of response or why does it attract that type of person?

George Vance Smith, a Unitarian, was a member of the Revision Committee chosen by Westcott and Hort. As a Unitarian, he did not believe in the deity of Christ. Other members of the committee passed a resolution that only those espousing this fundamental doctrine of Christianity could be allowed to work on the revision of the Bible. Westcott and Hort overruled their resolution, stating that if Smith were not allowed to work on the Revision, neither would they. Notice some of the interesting beliefs that were held by Smith.

He had doctrinal reservations regarding the deity of the Holy Spirit, the substitutionary atonement of Christ, and the inspiration of Scriptures. Here are his own words:

> ...what is really meant by the term in question [the Holy Spirit], is no other than God himself...but this fact will not justify us in saying that it is God the Holy Spirit, as though it were a distinct personality....

[Salvation] was in no way purchased of him [God] or of his justice. It was not because his "wrath" was appeased, or satisfied by the sufferings of an innocent substitute, but because of his own essential fatherly goodness and "great love." It is the "gift of God," not a thing bought from him with a price, except so far as this might be *figuratively* said in reference to that death of the Messiah.

…it is equally clear that it was not as their substitute that he died for men; not to redeem them from eternal misery; not…because the clouds of God's wrath had gathered thick over the human race, and required a victim, and could find that victim only in the innocent Jesus!…. The popular theory, in reality, is largely the product of dark and ignorant ages….

It is, that the Bible manifestly offers itself to us, the people of these later times, largely as a Book of History. It never professes or claims to be more: never, in truth, makes any profession or claim at all on that point; but stands before us there, simply as a collection of writings preserving for us the remaining literature, the traditions, and the history of the Hebrews…. It nowhere, in truth, claims inspiration, or says anything definite about it. The biblical inspiration, whatever it is or was, would seem, like the genius of Shakespeare, to be unconsciously possessed. The phrase, "Thus saith the Lord," and its equivalents, are simply to be referred to the style of the prophet; or to be understood only as indicating his belief that what he was about to say was conformable to the Divine Will…. It is scarcely allowable, in short, to think of inspiration as being or acting in the *dead works of any book*.[22]

Not only was George Vance Smith less than orthodox with his doctrinal reservations, he was also delighted with an opportunity to revise both the current Greek text and its subsequent authorized translation.

The only instance in the New Testament in which the
religious worship or adoration of Christ was apparently
implied, has been altered by the Revision: 'At the name
of Jesus every knee shall bow' [Philippians 2:10] is now
to be read 'in the name.' Moreover, no alteration of text
or of translation will be found anywhere to make up for
this loss; as indeed it is well understood that the New
Testament contains neither precept nor example which
really sanctions the religious worship of Jesus Christ.[23]

The old reading [God in 1 Timothy 3:16] is pronounced
untenable by the Revisers, as it has long been known to
be by all careful students of the New Testament.... It
is in truth another example of the facility with which
ancient copiers could introduce the word *God* into their
manuscripts,—a reading which was the natural result of
the growing tendency in early Christian times...to look
upon the humble Teacher as the incarnate Word, and
therefore as "God manifested in the flesh."[24]

Do you want to use a Bible that was revised by the false
doctrine and bias of this kind of man?

The two texts upon which *all* present-day Bible versions are
based differ greatly. They represent two entirely different schools of
thought and faith. If in this study, you are finding yourself favoring
the Received Text, then your Bible choice is fairly limited. The *only*
English Bible that emerges *solely* from the Received Text is the
King James Version of the Bible, and it is the only English Bible
whose text is free of modern day copyright restrictions in most of
the world.

Received Text

Textual criticism based on belief

5,600 Greek manuscripts give support

30,000 other manuscripts give support

Second-century vernacular Bibles support

Early church writings and lectionaries support

Based upon providential preservation

Guided by believers through the centuries

Supporters agree that it is accurate

Major English translation—KJV

Critical Text

Textual criticism based on unbelief

Less than 50 Greek manuscripts give support

Primarily based upon two disagreeing manuscripts

Manuscripts tie to Egyptian corruption

Accepted by cults and unbelievers

Developed in the mid-1800s

Primarily developed by non-Bible-believing men

Influenced by German rationalism

Supporters disagree among themselves

Based upon reconstruction of a supposed "lost text"

Chapter Seven In Summary

1. Westcott and Hort did not believe the Bible literally and had a preconceived bias against the Received Text.

2. Westcott and Hort invented a "Syrian Recension" and essentially explained away the vast body of evidence for the Received Text by asserting that the entire group of manuscripts came from the one "corrupt" source. They saw the majority as reason to doubt, yet we see the majority as God's unquestioned providence.

3. Received Text supporters have historically believed the Word of God literally, and believed it to be preserved and infallible. Critical Text supporters have historically believed the Word of God to be the work of men and have approached it allegorically.

4. Received Text supporters believe the manuscripts to be preserved from corruption while the Critical Text supporters view the manuscripts to be corrupted and needing protection from future corruption.

5. Both Tischendorf and Tregelles had limited exposure to ancient manuscripts, yet both claimed to have been able to discern thousands of changes necessary in their new Greek text based upon their studies.

6. The Critical Text is received today by a wider variety of doctrinal positions than the Received Text.

CHAPTER EIGHT

Understanding the Translations

One question must be answered. To whom did God give His Word? In 1 Timothy 3:15, we learn that the church is *"the pillar and ground of the truth"* (truth is God's Word according to John 17:17). In Jude 3, we learn that we are to *"contend for the faith* [body of beliefs] *which was once delivered unto the saints."* It is God's people that have the responsibility of propagating and defending God's Word.

When we reach a decision concerning which text is authentic, genuine, preserved, and used by Bible-believing churches through history, it is then time to choose a translation. Should you choose a King James Bible or a New King James Bible? Do you choose a New American Standard Bible or a New International Version? What about the English Standard Version?

You must give your attention to two particular and important areas regarding translation. First, you should consider the method that was employed by the translators. Second, you should consider the men who translated the Scriptures.

The Method of Translation

Methodology is based upon principles. Principles are based upon one's paradigm of truth. The methodology employed by the translators of the Authorized Version are radically different from the methodology used by the translators of the modern versions.

The Authorized Version committee was made up of fifty-seven men and divided into six companies. Each of these companies worked in different geographical areas.

Each company was divided and assigned its own sections of Scripture. Each individual translator was responsible to translate a portion of Scripture assigned to him. Once these individual translations were completed, the company assembled together in order to compare, discuss, and defend their work.

When a passage seemed obscure or difficult, additional "learned men" were consulted. Each book was reviewed and examined at least fourteen different times during the lengthy process. Contrast this with the New International Version Committee which boasted of going over each passage of Scripture *three* times during their translation process.

The technique employed by the Authorized Version committee is known as "formal equivalency" or "verbal equivalency." This meant that both the words and the forms of the words were rendered as closely as possible from Hebrew or Greek into English.[1] This is in distinction to "dynamic equivalency" used for the NIV—a belief that it is the message and thoughts, not the words, which are important.

It is readily apparent that the King James translators had a high view of God's Word. The manuscripts, previous English versions (such as the Geneva Bible, the Bishops Bible, and others), and sources in other languages were handled with care, and the new translation was meticulously reviewed multiple times in order to ensure fidelity to the underlying text. How does this method compare with the methodology used by the translators of our modern versions?

D.A. Waite explains it this way:

> Now the problem with all these other versions (including the NIV, NASB, NKJV) is that they have purposely selected a non-verbal equivalence type of translation, a non-formal equivalence type of translation, and a non-literal equivalence type of translation. Instead, to a greater or lesser extent, they have purposely adopted a dynamic equivalence type of translation. *Dynamic* implies *change* or *movement.* These various versions take a sort of idiomatic rendering from Hebrew or Greek into English. It is idiomatic in the sense that they didn't take a word-for-word method (even when it made good sense), trying to make the words in the Hebrew or Greek equal to the words in the English. Instead, they added to what was there, changed what was there, and/or subtracted from what was there. If it was a question, they might have made a statement, left out words, and so on.[2]

An illustration of dynamic equivalency can be found in Genesis 2:16–17 as well as Genesis 3:1. In chapter 2, we find the first command of God: *"And the* LORD *God commanded the man, saying, Of every tree of the garden thou mayest freely eat:"* (Genesis 2:16). In Genesis 3:1 and following, we find that Eve left out the word *freely.* Here she left something out, but claimed that it was what God had said. Later, she added a part about not even *touching* the tree in the middle. Eve both deleted and added to God's Word and took a liberty which was not rightfully hers. This is the same reasoning and risk behind the practice of dynamic equivalency.

The reason for dynamic equivalency is explained by the translators in the preface of the New International Version:

The first concern of the translators has been the accuracy of the translation and its fidelity to the *thought* of the biblical writers. They have weighed the significance of the lexical and grammatical details of the Hebrew, Aramaic, and Greek texts. At the same time, they have striven for more than a word-for-word translation. Because thought patterns and syntax differ from language to language, faithful communication of the meaning of the writers of the Bible demands *frequent modifications* in sentence structure and constant regard for the contextual meaning of words.

To achieve clarity the translators sometimes supplied words not in the original texts, but required by the context. If there was uncertainty about such material, it is enclosed in brackets. Also for the sake of clarity or style, *nouns, including some proper nouns, are sometimes substituted for pronouns*, and vice versa. And though the Hebrew writers often shifted back and forth between first, second, and third personal pronouns without change of antecedent, this translation often makes them uniform, in accordance with English style and without the use of footnotes.[3]

The philosophy behind the translators of the New International Version shows that the actual words used were *secondary* to the *thoughts* of the writers themselves. The priority should be given to the words of God, not the thoughts of men. The words of the Lord are pure words. God communicates His thoughts to us through words.

Furthermore, the translators of the New International Version took the liberty to substitute nouns and pronouns and change the person in which the writer was speaking—they did this without footnotes. *Now,* there is no way to tell what God had said as opposed to what these men have changed. The job of translators is to translate, not interpret.

The results of dynamic equivalency is that the translators become self-appointed interpreters, and in the end God's words are changed. For example, in the Today's English Version, *"the precious blood of Christ"* is changed to "costly sacrifice" in 1 Peter 1:19. Now I am not denying that His sacrifice was costly, but so was the spikenard poured out by Mary. There is a difference between the sacrifice of Mary and the precious blood of Christ.

The New King James Bible along with the New International Version and the New American Standard Bible change *"they knew him"* (KJV) in Mark 6:54 to "the people recognized Him" (NKJV and NASB) or "people recognized Jesus" (NIV). Now, was the meaning changed between these translations? Probably not! The issue is not always the meaning. Sometimes, it is the underlying notion that man thinks he can say something better than God originally said it. In what way does this change make the text better?

The New American Standard and the New International Version change *"him"* in Acts 25:3 to "Paul." Don Waite, in his book, *Defending the King James Bible,* has counted 2,000 examples of dynamic equivalency in the New King James Bible, 4,000 examples in the New American Standard, and 6,653 examples in the New International Version. The method of dynamic equivalence has become a license to change the words of God according to the whims of men.

The Men Behind the Translations

Not only are the methods of translation important, but so are the beliefs of the translators. While some would say that translation work is simply an academic exercise of placing one language into another—I believe that a translator's beliefs should be considered in reference to his translation work with the Word of God.

If someone is giving us God's Word in our language, it would be better for that person to understand that he is involved in a spiritual exercise, and not merely an academic task. Unquestionably, I prefer translators who believe in the infallibility of God's Word.

For those who translated the Authorized Version, a great book has been written already by Terrance Brown entitled, *The Learned Men*. While some would dispute the spiritual standing of these fifty-seven men, no one would dispute their respect for the Word of God, their education and scholarship, or their belief in the Bible as God's Word. Consider the one example of Lancelot Andrews—the man who oversaw the translation of the King James Bible. He had a manual for his private devotions prepared entirely in the Greek language. It was said that he was conversant in fifteen languages and that had he been present at the Tower of Babel, he would have served as the Interpreter General.

John Bois was another man who worked on this committee. By the time he was five years old, he could read the Old Testament in its entirety in Hebrew. At the age of six, he could write the Hebrew language eloquently.

These were remarkable men of their day and highly qualified to handle the task of giving the English world an Authorized Version.

How does this compare with the men who translated the Revised Version and its underlying Greek text? How does it compare with those who have been involved in the modern translations of our day? Is it possible to assemble men with this intellectual attainment, this type of orthodox doctrine, and this type of commitment to the Word of God?

Westcott, from his own writings in *Life and Letters of Brooke Foss Westcott*, denied the doctrine of creation. "No one now, I suppose, holds that the first three chapters of Genesis, for example, give a literal history—I could never understand how any one reading them with open eyes could think they did…."[4]

He doubted the historical existence of Moses and David. "If you feel now that it was, to speak humanly, necessary that the Lord should speak of the 'sun rising,' it was no less necessary that He should use the names 'Moses' and 'David' as His contemporaries used them."[5]

He was vague, if not heretical, in his view of the resurrection. "However much I may wish to maintain that the Resurrection and the Ascension are both facts, yet am I forced to admit that they are *facts wholly different in kind,* and for us the historical life of the Lord closes with the last scene on Olivet, though I do not forget the revelations of St. Stephen and St. Paul."[6]

Furthermore, on this same subject, he wrote concerning John 2:19, "On the other hand the *resurrection of Christ* was the raising again of the Temple, the *complete restoration of the tabernacle of God's presence to men,* perpetuated in *the church, which is Christ's body.*"[7]

Westcott also distorted the doctrine of inspiration. "In whatever way God made Himself known to them, they were His messengers, *inspired* by His Spirit, not in their words only but as men...."[8]

It is also apparent from Westcott's writings that he promoted a belief in baptismal regeneration. In writing on 1 John 5:6, he stated, "...and by His baptism Christ fulfilled for the humanity which He took to Himself, though not for Himself, *the condition of regeneration* [emphasis added]."[9]

Westcott also confused the doctrine of salvation. "If, then, we may represent suffering as the necessary consequence of sin, so that the sinner is in bondage, given over to the Prince of Evil, till his debt is paid, may we not represent to ourselves our Lord as taking humanity upon Him, and as man paying this debt—*not as the debt of the individual, but as the debt of the nature which He assumed* [emphasis added]."[10]

Closely connected with his view of salvation was his understanding of the doctrine of the atonement. "Would it be well to point out...that there has never been any authoritative theory of the atonement laid down in our Church, or in any of the historic Churches? The *fact* that Jesus died for our sins and for the whole world is firmly held, and we endeavor to see what lights this fact throws upon our own state and our relations to God and man."[11]

Hort does not fare much better as you study his positions doctrinally. Hort stated that he unequivocally believed in baptismal regeneration. "…we maintain Baptismal Regeneration as the most important of doctrines."[12]

Hort criticized those that were committed to systematic Bible reading. "…bibliolaters, among whom reading so many 'chapters' seems exactly to correspond to the Romish superstition of telling so many dozen beads on a rosary."[13] (If it is not important to read the Bible every day, why bother to translate it in the first place?)

Hort objected to the doctrine of eternal punishment. "Nor do I see how to dissent from the equally common Universalist objection, that finite sins cannot deserve an infinite punishment."[14]

He also called the substitutionary atonement a "heresy." In his words, "…that underlies the corresponding heresy (as it appears to me) of a fictitious substituted *penalty!*"[15]

Again, "I confess I have no repugnance to the primitive doctrine of a ransom paid to Satan, though neither am I prepared to give full assent to it. But I can see no other possible form in which the doctrine of a ransom is at all tenable; anything is better than the notion of a ransom paid *to the Father* [emphasis his]."[16]

Here is yet another of Hort's statements on his view of atonement: "I entirely agree—correcting one word—with what you there say on the Atonement, having for many years believed that 'the absolute union of the Christian (or rather, of man) with Christ Himself' is the spiritual truth of which the popular doctrine of substitution is an immoral and material counterfeit. But I doubt whether that answers the question as to the nature of the satisfaction. Certainly nothing can be more unscriptural than the modern limiting of Christ's bearing our sins and sufferings to His death; but indeed that is only one aspect of an almost universal heresy."[17]

Hort also claimed his lack of understanding concerning the doctrine of the blood atonement. He wrote: "…and finally St. Paul's mysterious words, 'Without shedding of blood there is no remission of sins.' But I have labored so utterly in vain to apprehend in any measure what this idea is, that I hope you will deepen and widen the hints you have already given."[18] We clearly see in these quotes a man very confused doctrinally and one who did not understand even the basic fundamental doctrines of God's Word.

It is also evident from Hort's writings that he concurred with Darwin's theory of evolution. "But the book which has most engaged me is Darwin. Whatever may be thought of it, it is a book that one is proud to be contemporary with. I must work out and examine the argument more in detail, but at present my feeling is strong that the theory is unanswerable."[19]

Finally, it is evident that Hort encouraged the exploration of Mariolatry. "I have been persuaded for many years that Mary-worship and 'Jesus'-worship have very much in common in their causes and their results."[20]

Consider the quotes you just read and realize that they were made by a man who is one of the two men who introduced the Critical Text to the world. His text, as previously stated, has either led to or directly influenced every new modern Bible version in existence today.

One final man to study concerning the Bible version question is S. Franklin Logsdon (1907–1987). He was a respected evangelical pastor and popular Bible conference speaker. He pastored Moody Memorial Church in Chicago (from 1950 to 1952). Prior to that he pastored Central Baptist Church in London, Ontario (from 1942–1950). He also pastored churches in Holland, Michigan (Immanuel Baptist from 1952–1957), and Erie, Pennsylvania. He taught at London Bible Institute in Ontario, Canada. He preached at Bible conferences (such as Moody Founder's Week) with well-known evangelists and pastors such as Billy Graham and Paul Smith of

People's Church in Toronto. Logsdon authored a number of popular books and commentaries published by Zondervan Publishing House. A notice on the cover of his book *Lest Ye Faint* states, "One of the most popular and best loved pastors is the author of this book. Mr. Logsdon is an uncompromising defender of the faith once delivered to the saints, and each Sunday in Moody Memorial Church in Chicago, thousands of people gather to have their souls refreshed from the divine springs of Christian truth." Logsdon was commissioned to do a feasibility study for the New American Standard, interviewed the translators, and even wrote the forward. Here is his testimony:

> As an honorary member of the Lockman Foundation, producers of the Amplified New Testament and the New American Standard Bible, I was invited to California back in the fifties to do a feasibility on utilizing the copyright of the 1901 which was as loose as a fumbled football. I was delighted and went.
>
> When it was decided to proceed with a revised publication, I assisted Mr. Lockman in interviewing a few of the men who served as "translators." What was finally used as the foreword was taken from the feasibility report written before the actual work had begun. Apart from this I had little to do with its production.
>
> Incidentally, you *cannot* get a list of the names of the "translators." Forbidden!
>
> I received #7 of the Deluxe copies, but did not for years even look inside it. It was too cumbersome to carry with me on the road. When questions began to reach me [pertaining to the NASB], at first I was quite offended. However, in attempting to answer, I began to sense that something was not quite right about the NASB. Upon investigation, I wrote my very dear friend, Mr. Lockman, explaining that I was forced to renounce all attachment to the NASB.

...I can aver that the project was produced by thoroughly sincere men who had the best of intentions. The product, however, is grievous to my heart and helps to complicate matters in these already troublous times.[21]

Again, in writing to David Otis Fuller, Logsdon makes a similar statement. "As a member of the editorial committee in the production of the Amplified New Testament, we honestly and conscientiously felt it was a mark of intelligence to follow Westcott and Hort. Now, what you have in these books [Dr. Fuller's books: *Which Bible* and *True or False*] strikes terror to my heart. It proves alarmingly that being conscientiously wrong is a most dangerous state of being. God help us to be more cautious lest we fall into the snares of the arch deceiver."[22]

On October 15, 1973, Logsdon again wrote Dr. David Otis Fuller about his feelings toward the New American Standard Bible:

> Duke, think of it, conceivably, by virtue of circumstance, I was in a position to have prevented the publication of the NASB. I'm definitely certain I could have, had I had in my possession the facts I now possess. If I could have read to Dewey Lockman the enclosed paper when he called me out there to help him lay the groundwork for the NASB, because he was so exceedingly conscientious, and so desirous of honoring God and His Word, he most surely would not have launched forth in it. I may be in trouble with the Lord. I didn't know, but I should have known to qualify for so important and so serious a matter of putting out a volume and calling it God's Word.[23]

These statements came from a man on the committee to produce the New American Standard Bible. After researching the issue of texts and translations, his final conviction was that the King James Bible was the authoritative Word of God.

Chapter Eight In Summary

1. God gave His people in His church the responsibility of protecting and propagating His Word.

2. The King James translation committee was made up of fifty-seven men in six companies. Each company was in a different location.

3. These translators had a high view of God's Word and used formal equivalency as their translational method.

4. The translators of most new versions used a dynamic equivalency method of translation.

5. The men behind the King James believed the basic doctrines of the Word of God, while the men behind the Critical Text did not.

6. The King James translators scrutinized every passage at least fourteen different times. The NIV translators scrutinized each passage three times.

7. Frank Logsdon, one of the respected members of the New American Standard Bible committee later renounced his involvement and publicly stated that he believed the King James Bible to be 100% correct.

CHAPTER NINE

Whom Will You Trust?

A s we come to this final section, the title of the chapter says it all. Whom will you trust? To whom has Scripture been entrusted? Does Scripture even answer this question?

> *"The eyes of the LORD preserve knowledge, and he overthroweth the words of the transgressor."*
> —PROVERBS 22:12

> *"Have not I written to thee excellent things in counsels and knowledge, That I might make thee know the certainty of the words of truth; that thou mightest answer the words of truth to them that send unto thee?"*—PROVERBS 22:20–21

The Scriptures do speak as to the subject of the "trustees" of God's Word. First, we are told expressly that it is the believers' responsibility to "*contend for the faith which was once delivered unto the saints*" (Jude 3). This verse emphasizes that our body of beliefs has been once delivered, and will never be delivered again. It also emphasizes that it was delivered "to the saints." This truth implies preservation. This concept of the responsibility of each believer links closely with the biblical distinctive of the priesthood of each believer. We are responsible before God to tell the next generation about the truth of God's Word.

Just as the believer is responsible to preserve God's truth, so is the local church. Paul, in writing to Timothy, stated that the church was the house of God, and that it was the pillar and ground of truth (1 Timothy 3:15). The Scriptures, therefore, give evidence that the local church and the individual Christians within those churches are the trustees of God's Word.

What do the Critical Text scholars say? Are they in agreement with the scriptural principles declaring who the trustee should be for the New Testament? Compare what the Scriptures have stated along side of one modern scholar's beliefs:

> We need such approved workmen, who are trained in the biblical languages and theology, who can confidently and accurately take us to the original languages when we have questions about translations. This, of course, is necessary whether we look at only one translation or many. We all have questions and need the help of God-gifted pastors and teachers. This also points to the necessity of a rigorous Hebrew and Greek curriculum in our seminaries. In a day when many are going into the ministry without the ability to go to the original languages to answer the question of God's people, we must recommit ourselves to go to the original language texts.
>
> Our purpose...is *to reconstruct from all the witnesses available to us the text essentially preserved in all, but perfectly preserved in none.* It is evident from the historical evidence that God has providentially preserved His Word for the present generation. However, we do

not believe that God has preserved His Word perfectly and miraculously in any one manuscript or group of manuscripts, **or in all the manuscripts.** Therefore, in our study of the text *we work with all the manuscripts to compile a text closer to the original than any one manuscript or group of manuscripts* [emphasis added].[1]

It would appear that the ordinary Christian cannot know the validity of God's Word without an understanding of Greek or Hebrew. We are in danger of falling into a major error of the Catholic Church. Catholic doctrine teaches that only the clergy can understand and interpret the words of God and that the laity must simply accept what is told to them. Those who hold to the Critical Text position would do much the same to us today by requiring that any ordinary Christian must know the Greek and Hebrew and be able to work with "all the manuscripts" to be sure that they have the authentic Word of God.

This same scholar goes even further to say in his quote that the Word of God has not been perfectly preserved in any manuscript and that it is not to be found in all of the manuscripts. In other words, the Bible has still not been found, even with all of the translations today! He said that he worked with all of the manuscripts to compile a text closer to the original, but it is highly unlikely that he has seen all of the manuscripts.

It is clear that this man begins with the assumption that we don't have God's Word, we will never have God's Word, but we can at least get closer to what it once was in original form. In the discussion of the Bible versions there are really only two basic choices—God's Word has either been *preserved* or it needs to be *restored*.

Yet another scholar has a similar outlook: "...the truth of infallibility does not extend to the preservation of an infallible text, nor to an infallible lexicography, nor to infallible answers to all questions about authorship, date, sources, etc., nor to an infallible reconstruction of the historical situation in which revelatory events occurred and the books of the Bible were written. *Such questions God in His providence has committed to human scholarship* to answer; and often the answers must be *imperfect and tentative* [emphasis added]."[2]

(Amazingly, according to this statement, the concept of "the infallibility of God's Word" has absolutely no practical value to the Christian!)

Saints or scholars? While many of the scholars—who presume to tell us which portions of our Bible are reliable and which are not—are believers, many are unbelievers. Again, it is not wrong for a "saint" to be a "scholar." Yet, when the "scholasticism" becomes the final authority over the Bible, man has presumed to put himself in God's place.

There is no biblical support for supposing that scholarly experts have had committed to them Scripture that has been kept from the ordinary Christian.

Ian Paisley, in his *My Plea for the Old Sword*, sets the issue in its proper perspective:

> Let us get the matter right. The Bible is not the production of man but the product of God. It is the Word of God. It was not delivered unto the scholars—Greek, Hebrew or otherwise, but to the saints. "The faith which was once delivered to the saints" (Jude 3).
>
> God has delivered His Book to the custody, not of the scholars, the universities, colleges or seats of learning, but only to His saints.
>
> Can any ordinary saint who has no knowledge whatever of the original languages know what is a proper version of God's Word or which is absolutely reliable? The answer is "yes" or else Jude 3 is error. Jude 3 is not error but divinely revealed truth.
>
> The attempt to bamboozle the ordinary saints of God with irrelevant controversy must be demonstrated. The ploy to take from the saints their divinely appointed

role of custody of the Book and place it into the hands of scholars must be exposed for what it is, a device of the devil himself.[3]

The care and transmission of the Word of God was left to the believers within the local church. The importance of preservation is not to argue primarily over which Bible to use. The reason preservation is a Bible doctrine is connected to the believer's responsibility of propagation. We are commanded to get God's Word to the masses—a command that would be impossible if preservation was not a reality.

The King James Bible and its underlying Textus Receptus are found to be trustworthy and authoritative documents. They have been used with great confidence and great consequences for hundreds of years.

Pat Alexander states in *The Lion Encyclopedia of the Bible*, "Many of the Greek manuscripts contain a text of the New Testament which was standardized in the fifth century AD. The first printed edition of the Greek text came in 1516—in a form prepared by the Dutch scholar Erasmus. *Up until then no one had questioned the accuracy of this text* [emphasis added]."[4]

The manuscripts supporting the Received Text and the King James are widely acknowledged to be valid and legitimate—even by those who reach a different conclusion in the version debate. Again, the proponents of the Critical Text say, "…we are not attacking the King James version of the Bible, nor are we attempting to persuade people not to use the KJV. Many of us…use the KJV; it is preached in our chapel and used in many of our classes. *We believe it is the Word of God*, and we believe the TR and the Majority Text are adequate Greek texts. We exalt the KJV as a monumental and greatly used English translation of God's Word [emphasis added]."[5]

Why would a man who makes such a statement see a need to write books and take part in discussions that we need other Bible versions? If the King James Bible is a monumental English translation of God's Word—if it is the Word of God—then may we write books and promote dialog that increases our trust and confidence rather than defeating it. May we enter into efforts to preach it, live it, and propagate it rather than to replace it!

God has promised to preserve His inspired Word. Based on that promise, verbal inspiration demands verbal preservation. Consider what one preacher observed: "Those who would deny the need for verbal preservation cannot be accepted as being really committed to verbal inspiration. If there is no preserved Word of God today then the work of Divine revelation and Divine inspiration has perished."[6]

In conclusion, there are at least seven reasons why the Critical Text, and the translations which it supports, are not to be trusted.

1. **They weaken or deny vital Bible doctrines such as the deity of Christ.** In Colossians 1:14, the King James Bible reads, *"In whom we have redemption through his blood, even the forgiveness of sins."*

    The little phrase, *"through his blood,"* is left out of the New International Version and the New American Standard Bible. Yet, the blood is an essential part of salvation for without the shedding of blood there can be no remission.

    One writer shares this observation of weakened Bible doctrine:

    > A footnote in the 1901 ASV at John 9:38 illustrates the perverted theology of its translators. This verse says the blind man who was healed by the Lord Jesus Christ "worshipped Him." The Bible plainly says that God and God alone is to be worshipped (Exodus 20:3–5). Thus the fact that Christ received worship clearly proves that He is God. Note the clever way the American revisers attempted to overthrow the teaching of

this verse with their footnote: "The Greek word denotes an act of reverence, whether paid to a creature (as here) or to the Creator."[7]

2. **Their own proponents admit the uncertainty of their position.** Notice the admitted uncertainty of those who endorse the Critical Text Bibles as seen in these quotes:

> Thus the text, built up on the work of the nineteenth century, has remained as a whole unchanged, particularly since the research of recent years has not yet led to the establishment of a generally acknowledged New Testament text.[8]

> Thus, Matthew 4:9...few or no witnesses besides, agree with our text....[9]

> That there is always somewhat of an uncertainty in these inferences has already been remarked.[10]

> If in the judgment of the Committee the meaning of a passage is quite uncertain or obscure, either because of corruption in the text or because of the inadequacies of our present knowledge of the language, that fact is indicated by a note. It should not be assumed, however, that the Committee was entirely sure or unanimous concerning every rendering not so indicated.[11]

3. **Their sources agree on obvious error.** Consider this quote from Zane Hodges regarding the errors found in the Critical Text: "Another factor militating against an uncritical acceptance of the oldest manuscripts is that they show a capacity to unite behind readings which— even in the eyes of modern scholars—are likely to be wrong. John 5:2 is a case in point."[12]

4. **There was a preconceived bias against the Textus Receptus on the part of Hort.** We've already seen this quote from Hort's writings: "I had no idea till the last few weeks of the importance of texts, having read so little Greek Testament, and dragged on with the villainous *Textus Receptus....* Think of that vile *Textus Receptus* leaning entirely on late MSS. It is a blessing there are such early ones."[13]

5. **They create doubt and confusion about the reliability of the Word of God.** John William Burgon, an early voice of opposition to the Critical Text shared this observation in the late 1800s: "In the meantime, the country has been flooded with two editions of the New Greek Text; and *thus the door has been set wide open for universal mistrust of the Truth of Scripture to enter* [emphasis added]."[14]

   Wilbur Pickering, a defender of the majority text wrote, "The *mischief* has been incalculable. The Hort theory and text have been perhaps the most effective weapons used by those who have made it their concern to defend and propagate their unbelief in the infallibility and authority of Scripture…those conservative schools and scholars who have propagated Hort's theory and text (Nestle is essentially Hortian) bear a heavy responsibility for the growing doubt and disbelief throughout the Church. The 'neo-evangelical' defection on scriptural inerrancy is a case in point."[15]

6. **The methodology employed in forming them is untrustworthy.** Zane Hodges wrote:

   > Modern textual criticism is psychologically "addicted" to Westcott and Hort. Westcott and Hort, in turn, were rationalists in their approach to the textual problem in the New Testament and employed techniques within which rationalism and every other kind of bias are free to operate.

The result of it all is a methodological quagmire where objective controls on the conclusions of critics are nearly non-existent. It goes without saying that *no Bible-believing Christian who is willing to extend the implications of his faith to textual matters can have the slightest grounds for confidence in contemporary critical texts* [emphasis added].[16]

7.   **They are presumptuous, if not dishonest.** Consider this amazing statement found in the very preface to the NIV Bible: "Because for most readers today the phrases 'the Lord of hosts' and 'God of hosts' have little meaning, this version renders them 'the Lord Almighty' and 'God Almighty.' These renderings convey the sense of the Hebrew, namely, 'he who is sovereign over all the "hosts" (powers) in heaven and on earth, especially over the "hosts" (armies) of Israel.'"[17]

The above quote is a perfect example of how modern translation committees have presumed to interpret what God meant rather than translating what God said. God said *"the Lord of hosts,"* but because the translators felt that the reader wouldn't understand, they chose a different wording. They changed God's Word based on presumed reader preference rather than textual authority!

Nestle and Aland share the following statement regarding their Critical Text: "The number of these further readings was increased with successive impressions and important conjectures were also added."[18] Do you want a Bible that has "important conjecture" added?

Clearly looking at the promises of the Word of God, and comparing them with what history has demonstrated, the following conclusions must be made:

1. God has promised to preserve His Word.

2. He has made His church and its members the guardians of His Word.

3. This historic church has accepted the Traditional Text as authentic and used it predominantly.

4. An attempt to undermine the doctrine of preservation and the Received Text originated during the 1700s from within the liberal realm of Christendom.

5. Those who use a Critical Text and/or its modern translations recognize the King James is still an accurate translation of God's Word.

6. New Evangelicals recognize the truth that the KJV has been the Bible of fundamentalism.

7. If the Head of the church, Christ, gave His Words to the church and they received them; if this church made faithful copies of what they received and spread them; if the majority of manuscripts found in the region where Christianity began still support the KJV, then there is no need to believe that the church has been wrong for nearly 2,000 years.

I know that the Bible version debate will not cease until we stand before the Lord Jesus Christ. I know that people will point out that the King James translators themselves would not be opposed to a revision of their work. However, there is a difference in revising a translation by updating archaic words, and in framing a new text based on a completely different stream of manuscripts.

The KJV translators recognized the authority of the text they chose. Instead of asking, "Hath God said?"—these translators stated, "The LORD God hath spoken...."

In contrast, scholars and textual critics today and in recent decades have led Christendom not only in asking "Hath God said?" but also in concluding that no one can really know exactly what God said at all!

Proverbs 30:5–6 says, *"Every word of God is pure: he is a shield unto them that put their trust in him. Add thou not unto his words, lest he reprove thee, and thou be found a liar."*

I firmly believe that we have today a "more sure word" of prophecy that is tried, tested, true, and trustworthy. Those who have used it recognize it for its theological and literary value. Those who prefer something else often state that they accept the King James Version, while at the same time acknowledging uncertainty about their preference. If both sides see the Received Text as adequate and trustworthy, I submit to you—*why not use the King James Version of the Bible?* I suggest that we trust the Lord in His promises and providence, and use what He has given us!

Chapter Nine In Summary

1. The Bible question boils down to either trusting God or trusting (in many cases) unbelieving scholars.

2. The Received Text and the King James Bible are widely acknowledged to be reliable, even by those who also support newer versions.

3. The Critical Text supporters agree and admit that it contains errors.

4. The men and methods behind the Critical Text are not trustworthy.

5. The men behind the Critical Text were heavily biased and dishonest.

6. Modern-day translators ask "Hath God said…?" The King James committee believed "The Lord hath spoken…."

Common Misunderstandings

As we finish our journey together, I thought it would be helpful to briefly address some of the common objections and misunderstandings that are used to refute the King James position or that are used to mis-characterize this position.

As I stated earlier, there are good people who land on both sides of this issue, and quite often, in discussion, surface arguments arise that usually represent misunderstanding. I also stated earlier that, while on both sides of this debate, there are difficult questions, I am far more comfortable with the questions on the King James side of the debate than with the questions on the Critical Text side.

Let's examine a few common areas of confusion:

Common Misunderstandings Regarding the Defense of the King James Bible

1. False Statement: The King James Bible was based solely upon the Textus Receptus. This is a common misconception of the Critical Text position. The King James was not *solely* based upon the Textus Receptus as the TR formally came into existence in the sixteenth century. It was based upon the Received Text of the local New Testament churches through the centuries—a body of manuscripts that included the formally printed Textus Receptus.

Regarding Erasmus' Greek text, it is true that this printed body of text contains some readings from the **Latin Vulgate**, primarily because this text was one of the texts most accessible to Erasmus. But by his third edition he had corrected the corruptions by diligent comparison with sources supporting the Traditional Text. The historical fact is that Erasmus took issue with Catholic doctrine and he saw a need for a correct text. The Textus Receptus was formally brought together in the 1500s, yet throughout Christian history, there is a body of text (i.e., Byzantine, Traditional) as well as writings and early translations that all form a consistent witness to the true words of God.

The Critical Text and the Received Text only disagree approximately 7–10% of the time, but those disagreements are often significant, including the validity of entire passages. One purpose of this book has been to show the overwhelmingly strong case that where they disagree, the historical body of the Traditional Text should be trusted rather than merely the "oldest manuscripts."

DEFINING THE TERMS

Latin Vulgate: A translation made by Jerome in AD 382 based upon both Byzantine and Alexandrian manuscripts. It became the official translation for the Roman Catholic Church.

For example, the NIV Bible is more than 64,000 words shorter and the New King James more than 19,000 words shorter than the King James Bible. This is a significant loss of words—equivalent to a good size book of the Bible.

2. False Statement: The Textus Receptus didn't come into existence until the sixteenth century with the work of Erasmus. This is a misunderstanding of the King James opponents based upon the fact that Erasmus first *printed* what would eventually be called the Textus Receptus in the 1500s. Erasmus did not coin this term, but he did believe (along with centuries of faithful Christians) in a Received Text. The Received Text was in existence long before Erasmus although not in a single, bound volume.

3. False Statement: The Received Text has many disagreements in which the translators had to make difficult decisions. This is simply not true. In the 5,600 copies of Greek manuscripts that exist today, there is clear and overwhelming evidence as to the accurate words of God (99% consistency). In addition to these Greek manuscripts, there are over 30,000 manuscripts and versional copies in other languages (e.g., Latin, Coptic, and Syriac), as well over 1,000,000 quotations from the New Testament in lectionaries and writings of early church leaders. This totals more than 35,000 manuscripts that verify the authenticity of the Received Text and the King James Bible. The Bible is by far the most copied and historically validated "literature" in human history.

So, what about the differences? What did translators do with the areas where the Received Text varies?

The nature of the variations is the real question. Are we dealing with simple phrasing differences among identical meanings or are we dealing with doctrinal questions and differences that change our faith (i.e., *Our Lord and Saviour Jesus Christ* versus simply *Jesus*)?

The wonderful answer to this question is clearly seen when comparing Scripture with Scripture, and every time the King James position is strengthened. If you were to compare the Critical Text versus the Received Text you would discover many doctrinal and defining differences—differences that profoundly impact the foundations of Christian faith. Yet if you were to compare the manuscripts and writings of the Traditional Text among themselves you would find minor reading variations but not doctrinal differences.

In dealing with these variations, the King James translators carefully cross-checked these decisions to assure that the reading was validated by the historical record.

4. False Statement: The King James Bible has readings that are not in the original Greek manuscripts. This sounds like a strong argument at first but it quickly falls apart. First, no one has an original Greek manuscript, so this statement is impossible to verify. Second, while there are some readings not found in *existing* Greek manuscripts, they *are* found in early Latin, in other ancient versions, and they are verified by the writings of early church leaders.

Additionally, there are some readings in the King James Bible that have absolutely no Greek manuscript evidence anywhere on the planet simply because they are the best English expression of a Greek idiomatic phrase. These are very few in number and always relate to idiomatic expressions where the translators collectively verified the clear meaning of the Received Text manuscripts. This was a very guarded form of what KJV opponents would refer to as dynamic equivalency. The King James translators made these types of choices only when the differences in the languages *required* it, while the translators of new versions took much greater license.

Any time a translation is made between two different languages, translators are forced to make some dynamic choices, but this is not how we would describe the over-all approach of the King James translators.

Over and over again, the committees of newer translations have been embarrassed as the Nestle Greek text has made modern textual changes based upon recent papyri discoveries. These recent changes continually validate the readings of the King James Bible.

5. False Statement: Mark 16:9–20 is not found in the earliest manuscripts. The scholars who use this statement are leaving out some very important facts. The earliest manuscripts they are referring to are *Sinaiticus* and *Vaticanus*. It is critical to note that the age of these manuscripts cannot be authoritatively verified—it is educated guesswork. Even if the age is accurate, there are many historical records that give witness to this passage that date back earlier than these two manuscripts. Some modern Bibles leave this passage out or question it merely based upon these two manuscripts. Of the 5,600 extant manuscripts in existence, 620 of them contain at least the last portion of the Gospel of Mark, and of these, 618 contain these twelve verses. The *only two* that do not are Sinaiticus and Vaticanus.

Finally, and perhaps most importantly, both Sinaiticus and Vaticanus have *empty spaces* where this passage belongs, leaving many questions. Why would a scribe leave a space for a passage that didn't even exist? Why did he leave it out? There is obviously more to the story that we cannot know. The historical record clearly supports this chapter in Mark in its entirety.

6. False Statement: The King James Bible is copyrighted. For the purposes of protecting the text, the King James Version of the Bible was originally copyrighted and still is in the United Kingdom. The rights to print this Bible were granted to several publishing houses over the centuries. Today, however, for the rest of the world, the King James Bible text is free of copyright restrictions.

This entire approach is quite different from the copyrights held today on modern Bible versions. The modern versions are tightly controlled by secular publishing empires for the primary purpose of revenue.

In other words, you could print the King James Bible in your basement if you so desire, but if you choose to use more than 200 words from the NIV, you are subject to the approval of Ruppert Murdoch's publishing empire.

7. False Statement: The name *King James Bible* shows that this Bible is the work of men. The King James Bible was originally referred to as the Authorized Holy Bible in English of 1611—officially commissioned and authorized by King James.

8. False Statement: The King James Bible uses outdated English and therefore it is harder to read and understand than modern Bibles. The English language reached its literary peak in the early 1600s. While the English language has changed, it has primarily deteriorated since that time. The strength of the English used in the King James Bible is its precision, simplicity, and accuracy.

Regarding ease of reading, the King James Bible has a significantly lower average syllable count, making it more accessible to a beginning English reader than the newer Bibles. Recent evaluation shows the reading level of the King James Bible to be fifth grade, as a whole—many individual passages would be lower. The modern Bibles are shown to be between sixth and ninth grade levels as a whole.

The modern versions claim to increase readability when in reality, they often make readability *more difficult.* New versions often use elongated words where the King James does not. Consider this list of KJV words and their New King James Version counterparts:

Evil to *adversity, calamity, disaster, catastrophe, distressing*
House to *habitation*
Smell to *savor*
Give to *gratify*
Man to *mortal*
Old to *elderly*

Bones to *limb*
Judge to *vindicate*
Children to *descendents*
Little rivers to *rivulets*
Box to *flask*
People to *multitudes*
Ended to *concluded*
Deep to *abyss*
Taken to *seized*
Divider to *arbitrator*
Riotous to *prodigal*
Old men to *elders*
Hell to *hades*
Judgment hall to *preatorium*
Thoughts to *anxieties*
Throne to *residence*
Stranger to *captivity*
Pictures to *sloops*
Fat to *verdant*

This is just the short list, and I encourage you to compare for yourself. More importantly, read that list again and consider it from the mind of an elementary child or a person learning the English language! God truly has made His Word accessible.

The above list also shows the preferential bias of translation committees. Read the list again and ask yourself, "In what way is the new word *better* than the previous one?"

However, we must wrestle with a larger question than "ease of reading." In this "Reader's Digest Condensed Version" generation, do we want to weaken Scripture under the guise of making it more palatable to today's reader, or do we want to maintain the integrity of what God said, even if it means we have to occasionally define a word as we study it? The King James Bible has many words that a variety of readers will need to define. This does not mean they need to be changed.

Many of the changes in modern Bibles were necessitated by marketing and not by textual authority. Revisers would have you think otherwise, but the facts are simple: To market a new product, you must create dissatisfaction with an existing product. Where there was no need for a new stream of Bibles, marketers and publishers have created a need by telling Christendom that our King James Bible just doesn't have the best translations. This marketing effort demanded that revisers come up with word alternatives to give legitimacy to their claims and their occupations.

9. False Statement: The King James Bible committee did not have the manuscript evidence we have today and they translated from inferior original language texts. Again, this argument is based upon the discovery of a few purportedly "older" manuscripts. The weakness of this argument is that these manuscripts don't even agree with each other and their age cannot be reliably verified.

Consider it this way. In a court of law, the King James translators called to the stand a record that agreed with today's body of 5,600 varied witnesses. This record is amazingly unified in agreement (along with thousands of other manuscripts and ancient versions). Suddenly, nineteenth-century scholars entered the courtroom claiming that they had *two new witnesses* who had superior knowledge to the overwhelming testimony of 5,600. When the witnesses were called to the stand, their stories didn't even agree between them and actually had remnants of stories long since cast out by the court. The stories of these two witnesses contradicted each other thousands of times in the Gospels alone. In any courtroom, these witnesses would be dismissed because they impeach each other's testimony, and any jury would see the authority of the 5,600.

10. False Statement: The King James Bible has gone through many revisions. This is yet another misunderstanding of the nature of "revision." The most significant change was that the Apocrypha, which was originally included for historical reading, was quickly dropped from later editions. It was included in between the testaments and was never a part of the sacred text. The translators removed it so there would be no confusion as to the true Word of God. Some editions continued to include the Apocrypha until 1827.

In addition to this, since the original King James Bible, the spellings of words and the shapes of letters have changed considerably with the development of the English language. Printing processes have also dramatically improved. Revisions of the King James Bible have been related to printing errors and spelling changes.

Modern-day printings of the King James Bible are either the Oxford 1769 edition or the Cambridge edition. If you placed a 1611 version of the King James Bible next to a present-day edition, you would find substantially the same wordings. The older one would be more difficult to read because of the spellings of words, the shapes of letters, and the quality of the printing.

For example, while presenting this material to my church family, I brought a page from an original 1611 edition of the King James Bible to my pulpit. I asked the church family to open their Bibles and compare the reading. As I read the entire page out-loud, my church family followed along in their present-day King James Bibles. When I reached the end of the page, I asked how many differences we came across—and there were none. This is quite a contrast to the widely variant readings and textual omissions in the modern versions.

11. False Statement: The earliest editions of the KJV included footnotes that offered variant readings or translations. These are not included in today's printings. Also the translators added words in italics that were not in the textual readings. This is true, but must be understood in the context of the larger issue. The KJV translators were diligent to protect the truth of God, and these footnotes were added, not to cast doubt on the Scripture, but to address transparently and strengthen any area of translational concern.

The italicized words were added only where translators deemed them absolutely necessary to correctly translate a passage or phrase into English. They italicized these words because of their respect to the Word of God and their accountability to His people. The reader can easily distinguish between the translation itself and the words added for clarification in English. Neither of these issues in any way take away from the fact that the King James Bible is translated from the reliable and trustworthy Received Text—and in fact they strengthen the case of the integrity and commitment of the translators to "get it right." Finally, none of these footnotes or italics in any way related to the influence of the questionable Critical Text or its "distant relatives" that would so heavily influence translation work in the centuries to follow.

Common Misunderstandings about the King James Position

As I stated earlier, there are many "positions" on this issue, but it seems that there is a large body of Bible-believing Christian brothers who neither agree with the hard-line Critical Text position, nor the extreme King James position. It's not that these men are looking for a "gray middle ground of compromise" so much as that the Holy Spirit in their hearts witnesses against the errors of both extremes.

Many who graduated from Critical Text schools are very uncomfortable with the illogical and unbiblical reasoning and conclusions to which this position leads. They are also uncomfortable with the fact that newer Bibles do at least diminish and erode some of the major doctrinal foundations of authentic Christianity.

Yet, the King James position has been often distorted, maligned, and forced into a corner marked "extreme"—sometimes by deceptive, non-fundamental Christians, and other times by those who would take an extreme and harsh position. Unfortunately, this has caused many Bible-believing Christians to cautiously step away from the King James position for fear of being stereo-typed or mislabeled as extreme. As a result, many Bible-believing Christians have been left in "no-man's land" on this issue and have taken a moderate, non-confrontational approach simply because they haven't closely studied the issue and because they don't like what they see at the two opposing ends of the spectrum.

The very label "King James only" is one held up mostly by proponents of other English Bibles. The very term "King James" makes this position appear to be based upon the authority of a distant English monarch, which it is not. It is based upon the textual authority that went into the translation of the Authorized Version. I am not saying in this book that God's Word is not to be found in other languages or that the work of God around the world must be limited to the King James Bible. God has preserved and migrated His Word into many languages and cultures throughout human history.

The King James position as referenced in this book, simply means that as English-speaking people who believe in the promises and preserving power of God, there's simply no reason to use a newer Bible when God has given us a proven, accurate record of His Words already, and especially when newer versions have such an unsure foundation and so many clear doctrinal differences.

Hopefully this book has encouraged you to understand the history, the facts, and to choose your authority for God's Word. The following is a list of statements that are often used against people who stand for the King James Bible, but these statements are simply not true about the King James position.

1. False Statement: All King James people force other language cultures to use the King James Bible. We believe the King James discussion is simply about God's Word for English-speaking people.

However, it is interesting to note that providentially, English has become the *lingua franca* (a common language used as a "bridge" by speakers of difference languages) of the entire world. This is true of English as it was of Greek in Christ's day. English has become indispensable today as the common "bridge" language between people of different primary languages. It is a wonderful testimony of God's providence that this English Bible found its way around the world with the expansion of the British empire over hundreds of years, and that it continues to be the dominant Bible of the world's most dominant language.

2. False Statement: All King James people believe that the King James is advanced revelation or "second inspiration" and therefore negates all other Bibles in any language. The term "advanced revelation" is meant to imply that God "re-inspired" His Word and gave a new revelation, similar to the claims of the Mormons and Joseph Smith. This thinking *would be* cultic. The problem with this statement is that modern textual critics define inspiration and preservation differently than Bible-believing Christians.

What is the *practical* difference between a "divinely inspired Word of God" and a "divinely preserved Word of God"? None. If God both inspired and preserved His Word, then we can have the confidence that the preserved Word is equal to the inspired Word for all *practical purposes* today—they are one in the same. To believe otherwise is to claim that God inspired a perfect Word and then proceeded to preserve it imperfectly. This is illogical.

3. False Statement: All King James people believe that the Bible should be worshipped like God Himself. While the Bible states that God exalts His Word above His name (Psalm 138:2), we do not believe that the Bible should be worshipped as God is worshipped. This is a misrepresentation of our belief that God's Word should be our final authority.

4. False Statement: All King James people believe that a man can only be saved from a King James Bible. History records that God has blessed the efforts of good men who preached the true Gospel of Jesus Christ from other versions of the English Bible and from other Bibles throughout the ages. The doctrine of salvation in biblical Christianity can be found in many other Bible versions, although there is a weakening of the teaching in some versions. The key is that where these versions are faithful in representing truth in their wording, God's Spirit can and will use His Words to convict people of sin, righteousness and judgment.

There is, however, great danger where the modern versions corrupt or distort the message of salvation. The corruptions make the message more difficult to communicate. They also make it easier to promote the various doctrinal positions of other religions and cults.

This is not an exhaustive list, but it does highlight some of the more common misunderstandings and faulty arguments about the King James Bible. May God bless you as you prayerfully share these truths with those who would ask. May we share these things in the spirit of Christ for the purpose of strengthening a brother, and not merely for the purpose of winning a debate or strengthening a position in pride.

King James Bible

Translated from the Received Text

Formal equivalency translation

Translators who viewed God's Word supernaturally

Received by English-speaking Christians for 400 years

Based upon belief in a preserved Word of God

Based upon a text dating to the second-century

Protects key doctrines, especially Christ's deity

A complete record of God's Word

Fewer syllables for easier reading

Non-market-driven copyright status

Marketing doesn't create need for word changes

New Bible Versions

Translated from Critical Text or new "Majority Text"

Dynamic equivalency translation

Translators viewed the Bible as any other book

Received by many pseudo-Christians

Based upon a belief in a restored Word of God

Based upon a text created in the 1800s

Dilutes or deletes key doctrines, especially Christ's deity

Ongoing revision attempting to resemble God's Word

More syllables for greater reading difficulty

Market-driven copyright status

Marketing creates need for word changes

CHAPTER TEN IN SUMMARY

1. The King James was not based solely upon the Textus Receptus.

2. The Received Text is substantiated by more than 35,000 manuscripts found in various languages and from a multiplicity of cultures and eras.

3. There are more than 1,000,000 quotes from early church leaders that further support the Received Text.

4. Mark 16:9–20 is one of the most questioned portions of Scripture, but it is heavily supported by witnesses in both streams of text.

5. The modern versions increase the reading difficulty of the English Bible.

6. The King James Bible has undergone typographical revisions, not translational.

7. The King James position has been often misrepresented and exaggerated by extreme positions on both sides of the issue.

CONCLUSION

We have covered a lot of ground, and I pray that God has challenged your heart and strengthened your confidence in His promise to preserve His Word. Thank you for taking the time to study this matter carefully.

As Christians, we must agree on one thing—Satan, from the Garden of Eden until this very moment, is attacking and undermining the Word of God. His common practice is to question and distort the Word of God—he always has, and he will continue until his final judgment.

It doesn't take a scholar to understand the big picture of the Bible discussion. Don't let the difficult questions deter you or sideline you from the major issues at stake.

When we step back from the spiderweb of historical details and redundant terminologies in this sometimes endless debate, what do we see as the major conclusions of the matter?

Quite simply, there are two primary sources of Bible texts—the first-century church and the state church. Another way to say it would be Antioch and Alexandria. Yet another way—the text used by local church Christians for centuries and the text reconstructed a little over 125 years ago.

They cannot *both* be 100% correct.

Why? Because they disagree.

They disagree on many major points. They say very different things in many places. Only *one* source of text can be the correct source, and logic would conclude that the other source is an attempt—at least in the spiritual realm—to diminish the truth.

Given the historical facts, the promises of Scripture, the leading of the Holy Spirit, and the overwhelming mountain of evidence—I pray that you will make your choice for the proven text of God's Words.

Simply stated, I encourage you to use the King James Version of the Bible for three reasons: first, the KJV position is the most consistent position with what the Bible says about itself. (The Received Text is the only text that fits within the Bible's teaching about God's Word.) Second, this is clearly the most defensible position both scripturally and historically. The historical evidence alone speaks very loudly to this fact. Third, it is the most logical position when considering all the facts given.

As Bible-believing Christians, we must consider the Word of God when it states *"So mightily grew the word of God and prevailed"* (Acts 19:20). Again God said, *"But the word of God grew and multiplied"* (Acts 12:24). We also see, in the early days of Christianity there were those who intentionally corrupted God's Word, *"For we are not as many, which corrupt the word of God..."* (2 Corinthians 2:17).

Having read the evidence for these two sources of text, you must answer for yourself this question: which text fits the description "the Word of God grew and prevailed"? Which text was *obviously multiplied* throughout the world, and which was obviously rejected by the providential hand of God?

The very fact that so many over the centuries have opposed this Traditional Text and yet it has prevailed should provide a great foundation for our faith! One author said it this way, "If the Received Text is an inferior text, why would the Holy Spirit allow it to completely dominate the propagation of God's Word over the first 1,500 years of Christianity?"[1]

I pray that you will choose to place your unwavering trust in that which clearly has God's miraculous promise of preservation and blessing.

As you set this book down, please weigh the following questions very carefully:

Do you want an evolving Bible or a solid foundation?

Do you want a Bible that was lost for 1,800 years or the Bible that true Christians have approved, used, and proven for 2,000 years?

Do you want a Bible that takes significant steps away from doctrinal purity or do you want one that solidly protects the major tenets of our faith?

Do you want a Bible that settles confusion or creates it?

Do you want a Bible that removes doubt or raises it?

Do you want a Bible that was the product of men influenced by German rationalism with a deep personal bias or one that was the product of God-fearing men who had a deep awe and reverence for the words they were translating?

Do you want a Bible framed upon a few obscure manuscripts that were rejected for centuries or a Bible framed upon the majority of manuscripts that coincide with the historical trail of the true Christian church?

Do you want a Bible that will stay the same for the next twenty-five years or one that will undergo continual revisions as scholars find ongoing reasons to insert their interpretive changes?

Do you want a Bible that is freely accessible to the world or one that is copyright protected by popular Christian publishing houses, many of which are owned by secular corporations?

Do you want a Bible that works for many different "Christian" religions and cults, or one that clearly defines the faith once delivered?

Do you want a Bible that is preserved or one that is "being restored"?

Did God keep His promise or not?

That is the question you must determine before God. If He did, then I believe the King James Bible is the logical, most substantiated, and most time-proven choice for the infallible, authoritative, and preserved Word of God for the English language.

> *"Being born again, not of corruptible seed, but of incorruptible, by the word of God, which liveth and abideth for ever. For all flesh is as grass, and all the glory of man as the flower of grass. The grass withereth, and the flower thereof falleth away: But the word of the Lord endureth for ever. And this is the word which by the gospel is preached unto you."*—1 PETER 1:23–25

Many years ago in a Moscow theatre, a matinee idol by the name of Alexander Roskopov was converted while playing the role of Jesus Christ. He was in a play entitled "Christ in a Tuxedo." It was mockery of Jesus Christ as Alexander Roskopov was supposed to read two verses from the Sermon on the Mount. Then, he was to stop in the middle of that reading and say, "Get me my tuxedo and my hat."

Alexander began to read from the Sermon on the Mount and as he was reading, he read the words of Jesus, *"Blessed are the poor in spirit: for theirs is the kingdom of heaven. Blessed are they that mourn: for they shall be comforted."* As he continued that reading, he began to tremble. He came under conviction, just from reading the Bible. He lost his place and kept reading through Matthew 5, despite the coughs and stamping of the foot of his director backstage. He kept on reading and finally, Alexander remembered a verse he had learned as a young boy in the Russian orthodox church, and in the middle of the play, he cried out and said, "Lord, remember me when thou comest into thy kingdom." On that stage in Moscow, Alexander called out to Jesus Christ to be his Saviour.[2]

Why do I believe in these precious truths? Because they change lives like Alexander's. As you help others to know the truth of the Lord Jesus Christ, it is vital that you have confidence regarding the Word from which you speak.

May God bless you as you read it, study it, memorize it, preach it, teach it, share it, and live it. May you close this book and choose to reclaim a deep confidence in the true Word of God.

You have a Bible you can trust and you have a God who has preserved it supernaturally as "a more sure Word"!

NOTES

Chapter 1

1. J. Williams, ed., *From the Mind of God to the Mind of Man* (Greenville: Ambassador-Emerald Publishing, 1999), p. 106.

Chapter 2

1. George Ladd, *The New Testament and Criticism* (Grand Rapids: Eerdmans, 1967), p. 81.
2. W. Edward Glenny and others, *The Bible Version Debate* (Plymouth: Central Baptist Seminary, 1997), pp. 7, 81.
3. Gordon Fee, *The Textual Criticism of the New Testament* in *Expositor's Bible Commentary*, Vol. 1, ed. Frank Gaebelein (Grand Rapids: Zondervan, 1979), p. 420.
4. Roy Beacham and Kevin Bauder, *One Bible Only?* (Grand Rapids: Kregel, 2001), p. 12.

5.   Ideas from this chart came from David Sorenson, *Touch Not the Unclean Thing* (Duluth: Northstar Baptist Ministries, 2001), p. 43.

Chapter 3

1.   Charles C. Ryrie, *Basic Theology* (Wheaton, IL: Victor Books, 1987), electronic media.
2.   Bernard Ramm, *Protestant Christian Evidences* (Chicago: Moody Press, 1957), pp. 232–233.

Chapter 4

1.   David Sorenson, *Touch Not the Unclean Thing*, p. 248.
2.   www.dbts.edu/pdf/shortarticles/statement.pdf—This statement was issued by the Detroit Baptist Theological Seminary in November 1996.
3.   W. Edward Glenny and others, *The Bible Version Debate*, p. 93.
4.   Gordon Fee, *The Textual Criticism of the New Testament*, p. 420.
5.   Roy Beacham and Kevin Bauder, *One Bible Only?* p. 109.
6.   W. Edward Glenny and others, *The Bible Version Debate*, p. 7.
7.   Robert Gromacki, *New Testament Survey* (Grand Rapids: Baker Book House, 1974), p. xii.
8.   W. Edward Glenny and others, *The Bible Version Debate*, p. 81.

Chapter 5

1.   Os Guiness, *Prophetic Untimeliness* (Grand Rapids: Baker, 2003), p. 54.
2.   Brooke Foss Westcott and Fenton John Anthony Hort, *The New Testament in the Original Greek*, American Edition, 1881 Edition (New York: Harper Brothers) p. 550.
3.   Ibid., p. 554.
4.   Ibid., 1896 Edition, pp. 122–124.
5.   Ibid., 1881 Edition, p. 560.

6. Ibid., p. 564.
7. Arthur Fenton Hort, *Life and Letters of Fenton John Anthony Hort*, Vol. 1 (New York: MacMillan and Co, LTD, 1896), p. 211.
8. William E. Ashbrook, *Evangelicalism: The New Neutralism* (Columbus: Calvary Bible Church, 1970).
9. John Ashbrook, *New Neutralism: Exposing the Gray of Compromise* (Mentor, OH: Here I Stand Books, 1992).
10. Ockenga wrote the foreword for Harold Lindsell's book, *The Battle for the Bible* (Grand Rapids, MI: Zondervan Books, 1976).
11. George Ladd, *The New Testament and Criticism*, p. 217.
12. Ibid., p. 80.
13. Os Guiness, *Prophetic Untimeliness*, p. 98.
14. Pamphet entitled, *Inspiration and Preservation of Scripture* explaining the position of Detroit Baptist Theological Seminary.
15. W. Edward Glenny and others, *The Bible Version Debate*, p. 71.
16. Ibid., p. 78.

Chapter 6

1. David Sorenson, *Touch not the Unclean Thing*, p. 258.
2. D.A. Waite, *Defending the King James Bible* (New Jersey: The Bible for Today Press, 2004), p. 56 and 41 respectively.
3. Definition taken from www.christiananswers.net/dictionary/vaticanuscodex.html.
4. http://rosetta.reltech.org/TC/extras/tischendorf-sinaiticus.html.
5. *Comparative New Testament: Old and New Versions Arranged in Parallel Columns* (Philadelphia: Porter & Coates, 1881), p. 9.
6. C.J. Ellicott, *Considerations on the Revision of the English Version of the New Testament* (London: Longmans, Green, Reader, and Dyer, 1870), p. 99.

7. C.J. Ellicott, *Addresses on the Revised Version of Holy Scripture* (Wipf & Stock, 2006), pp. 11–14.

8. Alfred Martin, *A Critical Examination of the Westcott-Hort Textual Theory* quoted in *Which Bible?* (Grand Rapids, MI: Grand Rapids International Publications, 1975), p. 60.

9. Arthur Fenton Hort, *Life and Letters of Fenton John Anthony Hort*, p. 431.

10. Martin, Dissertation for PhD from Dallas Theological Seminary, May 1951…quoted in *Which Bible?*, edited by David Fuller, p. 149.

11. F.H.A. Scrivener, *A Full Collation of the Codex Sinaiticus with the Received Text of the New Testament* (Cambridge: Deighton, Bell, and Co., 1864), p. xix.

12. R.L. Dabney, *The Doctrinal Various Readings of the New Testament Greek* (Carlisle, PA, USA: The Banner of Truth Trust, 1967), pp. 350–389.

13. Dean Burgon, *The Last Twelve Verses of the Gospel According to St. Mark* (Oxford and London: James Parker and Co., 1871), p. 87.

14. Dean Burgon, *The Traditional Text of the Holy Gospels Vindicated & Established* (Cambridge: Deighton, Bell and Co., 1896), pp. 11–12.

15. Thomas Strouse, *The Lord God Hath Spoken, A Guide to Bibliology* (Virginia Beach: Tabernacle Baptist Press, 1998), pp. 17–18.

16. C.J. Ellicott, *The Revisers and the Greek Text of the New Testament by Two Members of the New Testament Company* (London: Macmillan & Co., 1882), pp. 11–12.

17. Dean Burgon, *The Traditional Text of the Holy Gospels*, p. 16.

18. Dean Burgon, *The Revision Revised* (London: William Clowes and Sons, 1883), p. 269.

Chapter 7

1. Arthur Fenton Hort, *Life and Letters of Fenton John Anthony Hort*, p. 420.

2. Wilbur Pickering, *The Identity of the New Testament Text* (Nashville: Nelson, 1977), p. 41.

3. Jack Moorman, *Forever Settled: Survey of the Documents and History of the Bible*—posted online @ www.biblebelievers.net/bibleversions/kjcforv4.htm.

4. Terrance Brown, *What is Wrong with the Modern Versions of the Holy Scriptures?* Article No. 41 (Trinitarian Bible Society, 1971).

5. Dean Burgon, *Revision Revised*, 1885.

6. W. Edward Glenny and others, *The Bible Version Debate*, pp. 43–44.

7. Westcott and Hort, *New Testament in the Original Greek*, p. 235.

8. Gordon Fee, *Textual Criticism of the New Testament*, p. 420.

9. Arthur Fenton Hort, *Life and Letters of Fenton John Anthony Hort*, pp. 280–281.

10. Posted online @ www.biblebelievers.net/bibleversions/kjcforv5.htm

11. "Origen" McClintock and Strong, Encyclopedia.

12. F.H.A. Scrivener, *A Plain Introduction to the Criticism of the New Testament* (Cambridge: Deighton, 1861), p. 386.

13. Terrance Brown, *What is Wrong with the Modern Versions?* Article No. 41.

14. Dean Burgon, *Revision Revised*, p. 30.

15. B.H. Streeter, *The Four Gospels: A Study of Origins* (New York: Macmillan and Co., 1924), p. 131.

16. H.S. Miller, *General Biblical Introduction* (Houghton, NY: Word-Bearer Press, 1960), pp. 184–185.

17. Benjamin B. Warfield, *An Introduction to the Textual Criticism of the New Testament* (London: Hodder and Stoughton, 1886), p. 12.

18. Dean Burgon, *Traditional Text of the Holy Gospels*, pp. 241, 243.

19. This quote is taken from a web page: http://rosetta.reltech. org/TC/extras/tischendorf-sinaiticus.html, which is an extract from *When Were Our Gospels Written? An Argument by Constantine Tischendorf. With a Narrative of the Discovery of the Sinaitic Manuscript* (New York: American Tract Society, 1866) by Tischendorf.

20. David Otis Fuller, *True or False* (MI: Grand Rapids International Publications, 1973), pp. 71–72.

21. George S. Bishop, *The Doctrines of Grace and Kindred Themes* (New York: Gospel Publishing House, 1910).

22. George Vance Smith, *The Bible and Its Theology* (London: S. Sonnenschein & Co., 1892), Each of the four paragraphs given are from this book. Paragraph 1 is from p. 215. Paragraph 2 is from 246. Paragraph 3 comes from pages 248 and 253. The final paragraph is from pages 269, and 276–277.

23. George Vance Smith, *Texts and Margins of the Revised New Testament Affecting Theological Doctrine* (London: British and Foreign Unitarian Association, 1881), p. 47.

24. Ibid., p. 39.

Chapter 8

1. D.A. Waite, *Defending the King James Bible*, pp. 83–90.

2. Ibid., pp. 89–90.

3. Both quotations are taken from the preface to the New International Version, page xvi and xviii respectively. Emphasis not found in the original.

4. Brooke Foss Westcott, *Life and Letters of Brooke Foss Westcott,* Vol. 2 (MacMillan and Co., London, 1903), p. 69.

5. Ibid.

6. Brooke Foss Westcott, *Life and Letters,* Vol. 1, p. 287.

7. Brooke Foss Westcott, *The Gospel According to St. John: The Authorized Version with Introduction and Notes,* Vol. 1 (London: John Murray, 1882), p. 42.

8. Brooke Foss Westcott, *Epistle to the Hebrews: The Greek Text with Notes and Essays* (London: Macmillan, 1903), p. 6.

9. Brooke Foss Westcott, *Epistles of St. John: the Greek Text with Notes and Addenda* (London: Macmillan, 1892), p. 181.

10. Brooke Foss Westcott, *Life and Letters,* Vol. 1, p. 239.

11. Ibid, Vol. 2, p. 226.

12. A.F. Hort, *Life and Letters of Fenton John Anthony Hort,* Vol. 1, p. 76.

13. Ibid., p. 77.

14. Ibid., p. 118.

15. Ibid., p. 120.

16. Ibid., p. 428.

17. Ibid., p. 430.

18. Ibid., p. 122.

19. Ibid., p. 416.

20. Ibid., Vol. 2, p. 50.

21. S. Franklin Logsdon, Letter to Cecil Carter of Prince George, British Columbia: June 9, 1977.

22. S. Franklin Logsdon, Letter to David Fuller, September 5, 1973.

23. S. Franklin Logsdon, Letter to David Fuller, October 15, 1973.

Chapter 9

1. W. Edward Glenny and others, *The Bible Version Debate,* pp. 122, 131.

2. George Ladd, *The New Testament and Criticism,* p. 217.

3. Ian Paisley, *My Plea for the Old Sword* (Ambassador-Emerald Publishing, 1997), pp. 75–76.

4. Pat Alexander, ed., *The Lion Encyclopedia of the Bible*, Lion Publishing Corporation (reprinted by Reader's Digest Association, Inc., 1987) p. 70.

5. W. Edward Glenny and others, *The Bible Version Debate*, p. 129.

6. Ian Paisley, *My Plea for the Old Sword*, p. 103.

7. David Cloud, *For Love of the Bible* (Port Huron: Way of Life Literature), p. 38.

8. Erwin Nestle and Kurt Aland, eds., *Novum Testamentum Graece*, p.60.

9. Ibid., p. 78.

10. Ibid., p. 79.

11. Preface to the Revised Standard Version, p. vi.

12. Zane Hodges, quoted in *Which Bible?*, p. 29.

13. A.F. Hort, *Life and Letters*, p. 211.

14. Dean Burgon, *Revision Revised*, Preface, p. xxx.

15. Wilbur Pickering, quoted in *True or False*, p. 279.

16. Zane Hodges, *Rationalism and Contemporary New Testament Textual Criticism* (Bibliotheca Sacra, Jan 1971), pp. 27–35.

17. Preface to the NIV, p. xvii.

18. Nestle and Aland, *Novum Testamentum Graece*, p. 60.

Conclusion

1. David Sorenson, *Touch not the Unclean Thing*, p. 83.

2. This illustration was originally given on page 121 in *Why Christians Sin*, by J.K. Johnston (Grand Rapids, MI: Discovery House Publishers, 1992). The illustration is also found online at http://net.bible.org/illustration.php?topic=160 as well as http://www.bible.org/illus.php?topic_id=160.

BIBLIOGRAPHY

Alexander, Pat. ed. *The Lion Encyclopedia of the Bible.* Lion Publishing Corporation (reprinted by Reader's Digest Association, Inc., 1987)

Ankerberg, John, and John Weldon. *The Facts on the King James Only Debate.* Eugene, OR: Harvest House Publishers, 1996

Archer, Gleason. *A Survey of Old Testament Introduction.* Chicago, IL: Moody, 1964

Ashbrook, John. *New Neutralism: Exposing the Gray of Compromise.* Mentor, OH: Here I Stand Books, 1992

Ashbrook, William E. *Evangelicalism: The New Neutralism.* Columbus: Calvary Bible Church, 1970

Bainton, Roland. *Here I Stand.* New York: Abingdon Press, 1950

Bancroft, Emery. *Elemental Theology.* Grand Rapids, MI: Kregel Publications, 1996 (reprint)

Barker, Ken. *Accuracy Defined and Illustrated.* Colorado Springs, CO: International Bible Society, 1995

Barr, James. *Fundamentalism.* London: SCM Press Ltd., 1977

Beacham, Roy, and Kevin Bauder. *One Bible Only?* Grand Rapids, MI: Kregel Publications, 2001

Bere, M. *Bible Doctrines for Today.* Pensacola, FL: A Beka, 1987

Bishop, George S. *The Doctrines of Grace and Kindred Themes.* New York: Gospel Publishing House, 1910

Borg, M. *The Heart of Christianity.* San Francisco: Harper, 2003

Brown, Terrance. *What is Wrong with the Modern Versions of the Holy Scriptures?* Article No. 41, Trinitarian Bible Society, 1971

Bruce, F.F. *The Books and the Parchments.* Old Tappen: Revell, 1963

Burgon, Dean. *The Revision Revised.* London: William Clowes and Sons, 1883

———*The Last Twelve Verses of the Gospel of St. Mark.* Oxford and London: James Parker and Co., 1871

———*The Traditional Text of the Holy Gospels Vindicated & Established.* Cambridge: Deighton, Bell and Co., 1896

Calvin, John. *Institutes in Christian Religion.* Vol. 1

Campbell, J.L. *The Bible Under Fire.* Joplin, MO: College Press, 1928

Carson, D.A. *The King James Version Debate: A Plea for Realism.* Grand Rapids, MI: Baker Book House, 1979

Carter, Mickey P. *Things that are Different are not the Same.* Haines City, FL: Landmark Baptist Press, 1993

Clarke, Donald. *Bible Version Manual.* Millersburg, PA: B.T.M. Publications, 1975

Cloud, David. *For Love of the Bible.* Port Huron: Way of Life Literature

Colwell, E.C. *What is the Best New Testament?* Chicago, IL: University of Chicago Press, 1952

Comparative New Testament: Old and New Versions Arranged in Parallel Columns. Philadelphia: Porter & Coates, 1881

Dabney, R.L. *The Doctrinal Various Readings of the New Testament Greek.* Vol. 1. Carlisle, PA, USA: The Banner of Truth Trust, 1967

Ellicott, C.J. *Addresses on the Revised Version of Holy Scripture*. Wipf & Stock, 2006 (Previously published by SPCK, 1901)

———*Considerations on the Revision of the English Version of the New Testament*. London: Longmans, Green, Reader, and Dyer, 1870

——— *The Revisers and the Greek Text of the New Testament by Two Members of the New Testament Company*. London: Macmillan & Co., 1882

Fee, Gordon. *The Textual Criticism of the New Testament* in *Expositor's Bible Commentary*. ed. Frank Gaebelein (Grand Rapids: Zondervan, 1979

Fuller, David Otis. *True or False?* MI: Grand Rapids International Publications, 1973

———*Which Bible?* Grand Rapids, MI: Grand Rapids International Publications, 1975

Geisler, N.L., and W.E. Nix. *From God to Us*. Chicago, IL: Moody Press, 1981

Glenny, W. Edward, and others. *The Bible Version Debate: The Perspective of Central Baptist Seminary*. Minneapolis, MN: Central Baptist Seminary, 1997

Grady, Dr. William P. *Final Authority: A Christian's Guide to the King James Bible*. Schererville, Indiana: Grady Publications, 1993

Gromacki, Robert. *New Testament Survey*. Grand Rapids: Baker Book House, 1974

Guiness, Os. *Prophetic Untimeliness*. Grand Rapids: Baker, 2003

Hills, Edward F. *The King James Version Defended*. Des Moines, Iowa: The Christian Research Press, 1984

Hodges, Zane. *Rationalism and Contemporary New Testament Textual Criticism*. Bibliotheca Sacra, Jan 1971

Hort, Arthur Fenton. *Life and Letters of Fenton John Anthony Hort*. I:419–421. Westcott and Hort II

Johnston, J.K. *Why Christians Sin*. Grand Rapids, MI: Discovery House Publishers, 1992

Josephus. *The Complete Works of Josephus*. Grand Rapids, MI: Kregel, 1981

Kaiser, Walter Jr. *Introduction to Biblical Hermeneutics*. Grand Rapids, MI: Zondervan Publications, 1994

Kenyon, F. *The Story of the Bible*. London: John Murray, 1944

————*The Bible and Archaeology*. New York: Harper & Brothers, 1940

Ladd, George. *The New Testament and Criticism*. Grand Rapids: Eerdmans, 1967

Letis, Theodore P. *A New Hearing For The Authorized Version*. Philadelphia, PA: The Institute for Renaissance and Reformation Biblical Studies, 1997

Lindsell, Harold. *The Battle for the Bible*. Grand Rapids, MI: Zondervan Books, 1976

Lockyer, Dr. Herbert. *All the Doctrines of the Bible*. Grand Rapids, MI: Zondervan Books, 1964

Martin, Alfred. *A Critical Examination of the Westcott-Hort Textual Theory*. Quoted in *Which Bible?* Second edition, page 253

Miller, H.S. *General Biblical Introduction*. Houghton, NY: Word-Bearer Press, 1960

Nestle, Erwin, and Kurt Aland, eds. *Novum Testamentum Graece*

Nolan, Frederick. *An Inquiry into the Integrity of the Greek Vulgate*. London: 1815

Packer, J.I. *God Speaks to Man*. London, England: Hodder and Stroughton, 1965

Paisley, Ian. *My Plea for the Old Sword*. Ambassador-Emerald Publishing, 1997

Pardington, George P. *Outline Studies in Christian Doctrine*. Harrisburg, PA: Christian Publications, Inc., 1926

Phillips, John. *Exploring the Word of the Jew*. Chicago: Moody , 1927

Pickering, Wilbur. *The Identity of the New Testament Text*. Nashville: Nelson, 1977

Ramm, Bernard. *Protestant Christian Evidences*. Chicago: Moody Press, 1957

Ryrie, Charles C. *Basic Theology.* Wheaton, IL: Victor Books, 1987, electronic media

Sargent, Robert. *Landmarks of Baptist Doctrine.* Oak Harbor, WA: Bible Baptist Publications

Saucy, Robert L. *The Bible: Breathed from God.* Wheaton, IL: Victor Books, 1973

Scrivener, F.H.A. *A Supplement to the Authorized English Version of the New Testament: Being a Critical Illustration of its More Difficult Passages from the Syriac, Latin, and Earlier English Versions, with an Introduction.* London: William Pickering, 1845

———*A Full Collation of the Codex Sinaiticus with the Received Text of the New Testament.* Cambridge: Deighton, Bell, and Co., 1864

———*A Plain Introduction to the Criticism of the New Testament.* Cambridge: Deighton, 1861

———*Bezae Codex Cantabrigiensis: being an exact Copy, in ordinary Type, of the celebrated Uncial Graeco-Latin Manuscript of the Four Gospels and Acts of the Apostles, written early in the Sixth Century, and presented to the University of Cambridge by Theodore Beza A.D. 1581. Edited, with a critical Introduction, Annotations, and Facsimiles.* Cambridge, 1864

———*Six Lectures on the Text of the New Testament and the ancient MSS. which contain it, chiefly addressed to those who do not read Greek.* Cambridge and London, 1875

———*The New Testament in the Original Greek according to the Text followed in the Authorized Version, together with the Variations adopted in the Revised Version. Edited for the Syndics of the Cambridge University Press, by F.H.A. Scrivener, M.A., D.C.L., L.L.D., Prebendary of Exeter and Vicar of Hendon.* Cambridge: Cambridge University Press, 1881

Smith, George Vance. *The Bible and Its Theology.* London: S. Sonnenschein & Co., 1892

————*Texts and Margins of the Revised New Testament Affecting Theological Doctrine.* London: British and Foreign Unitarian Association, 1881

Sorenson, David. *Touch Not The Unclean Thing: The Text Issue and Separation.* Duluth, MN: Northstar Baptist Ministries, 2001

Streeter, B.H. *The Four Gospels: A Study of Origins.* New York: Macmillan and Co., 1924

Strouse, Thomas M. *"But My Words Shall Not Pass Away": The Biblical Defense Of The Doctrine Of The Preservation Of Scripture.* Newington, CT: Emmanuel Baptist Theological Press, 2001

————*The Lord God Hath Spoken: A Guide to Bibliology.* Virginia Beach, VA: Tabernacle Baptist Theological Press, 1998

Surrett, Charles L. *Which Greek Text?: The Debate Among Fundamentalists.* Kings Mountain, NC: Surrett Family Publications, 1999

Torrey, R.A. *The Importance and Value of a Proper Bible Study.* New York: George H. Doran Co., 1921

Waite, D.A. *Defending the King James Bible: A Four-fold Superiority.* Collingswood, NJ: Bible for Today, 1992

Warfield, Benjamin B. *An Introduction to the Textual Criticism of the New Testament.* London: Hodder and Stoughton, 1886

Wesley, John. *Notes on the Old and New Testaments.* Power Bible CD: Online Publishing

Westcott, Brooke Foss. *Life and Letters of Brooke Foss Westcott.* Vol. 2 MacMillan and Co., London, 1903

————*The Gospel According to St. John: The Authorized Version with Introduction and Notes.* 2 Vols. London: John Murray, 1882 & 1908

————*Epistle to the Hebrews: The Greek Text with Notes and Essays* 3rd Edition. London: Macmillan, 1903

————*Epistles of St. John: the Greek Text with Notes and Addenda.* London: Macmillan, 1883; other editions in 1886 & 1892

Westcott, Brooke Foss, and Fenton John Anthony Hort, *The New Testament in the Original Greek*. American Edition, New York: Harper Brothers, 1881

White, James R. *The King James Only Controversy*. Minneapolis, MN: Bethany House Publishers, 1995

Williams, J., ed. *From the Mind of God to the Mind of Man*. Greenville: Ambassador-Emerald Publishing, 1999

Wurthweir, Ernst. *The Text of the Old Testament*. Grand Rapids, MI:Eerdmans, 1981

Web Pages and a Brief Synopsis

www.aloha.net/~bstaggs/vrstbl/html. This site does not match its name. See chart entitled *All versions are not saying the same thing!*

www.bible.org/docs/soapbox/kjv_1611.htm. This article by Daniel Wallace shows the changes to the KJV since the 1611 edition.

www.biblebb.com/files/howbible.htm. This site is sponsored by Indian Hills Community Church. It is dedicated to teaching people how we received our Bible.

www.biblebelievers.net/bibleversions.kjcforv4.htm. This link goes to page 65 of a book compiled by Jack Moorman—*Forever Settled: A Survey of the Documents and History of the Bible*.

www.bibletexts.com/kjv-tr.htm#6. This site is dedicated to the promotion of the King James and the Textus Receptus.

www.blueletterbible.com. Earlier in the book, information was given about Johanan ben Zakkai and the Council at Jamnia.

www.carthage.lib.il.us/community/churches/primbap/Bible.html. This site is sponsored by a primitive Baptist church endeavored to show a history of their Bible.

www.christiananswers.net/dictionary/vaticanuscodex.html. Gives the definition of Codexis Vaticanus.

www.dbts.edu/pdf/shortarticles/statement.pdf. Statement issued by Detroit Baptist Theological Seminary November 1996.

www.earlham.edu/~seidi/iam/tc_codexs.html. This site is an educational journey into the world of "Sinaiticus."

www.ekkcom.com/gail17.htm. This link is a quick question about the Waldensian Bible and its connection with Calvin and Beza.

www.geocities.com/Heartland/Plains/8936/TEXTUS.HTM. This site could be subtitled "The Battle of the Bibles" as it seeks to document two competing streams of text.

www.geocities.com/paulmizzi/bib-tr.htm. This link gives an article entitled "The Preservation of the Textus Receptus."

www.kjvonly.org/doug/waldensian_pr.htm. Reprint of article by Kutilek from the Baptist Biblical Heritage 2:2, Summer 1991. Attempts to identify KJV-onlyism with Seventh Day Adventist, Benjamin Wilkerson. It is also an attempt to recast the Waldensian Bible's place in the history of the Traditional Text.

www.kjvonly.org/gary/variations_in_the_textus.htm. This site is sponsored by a man who uses the KJV, but takes the time to point out that there are variations within the Textus Receptus.

www.lg3d.com/bju/kjv.html. Gives the "unofficial" official position of Bob Jones University.

www.mun.ca/rels/restmov/texts/dasc/HWGIOO.HTM. Someone has taken the time to post an 1898 book by Charles Leach on the web. Title: *How We Got our Bible*, published by Fleming Revell.

www.newadvent.org/cathen/13722.a.htm. This "Catholic article" shows Jerome's Vulgate as an attempt to update the "corrupt" Itala being used by the people.

www.ntcanon.org/authorities.shtml This site features an article entitled "The Development of the Canon of the New Testament." Particularly, this site speaks about the early Christian authorities and their contribution to the developing text.

www.oracle2icoc.org/pages/Essential/EMore040.html. This site is a short page speaking about the illuminating work of the Holy Spirit in relation to the Word of God.

www.reformedreader.org/iofscriptures.htm. This site has part of a book written by B.H. Carroll entitled Inspiration of the Scriptures as Believed by Baptists.

www.robibrad.demon.co.uk/Spirit.htm. This site deals with inspiration and illumination of Scriptures.

www.rosetta.reltech.org/TC/extras/tischendorf-sinaiticus.html. This site is taken from a book by Tischendorf and displays his attitude toward the Traditional Text and his desire to reconstruct the original text.

www.skypoint.com/~waltzmn/uncialScript.html. This site compares the uncial script with other Greek writings.

www.sundayschoolcourses.com/origins/originsc.htm#_ Toc409530510. This site deals with the Church Fathers and the Bible from which they quoted. It is in a Sunday school format.

www.users.aol.com/libcfl/autogrph.htm. This site published by a church in Lubbock, TX uploads the work of David Otis Fuller.

www.wayoflife.org/fbns/historyevangelical.htm. Here is a reprint of a section of John Ashbrook's book: *New Neutralism: Exposing the Gray of Compromise.*

Periodicals and Essays

Buch, Mark. *In Defence of the Authorized Version.* Self-published, 1977

Flanders, Dr. Richard *Why we use the King James Version of the Bible.* Vassar, MI: Juniata Baptist Church

Keen, Charles. *A Short Essay of the English Bible.* Milford, OH: Bearing Precious Seed

Logsdon, S. Franklin. *Letter to Cecil Carter of Prince George.* British Columbia: June 9, 1977

———*Letter to David Fuller.* September 5, 1973

———*Letter to David Fuller.* October 15, 1973

Minnick, Mark. *Trusted Voices on Translations.* Greenville, SC: Mount Calvary Baptist Church

Strouse, Thomas. *From the Mind of God to the Mind of Men: A book review.* Newington, CT: Emmanuel Baptist Theological Seminary, Volume 1, Issue 2—November, 2000

——*The Pauline Antidote for Christians Caught in Theological Heresy.* Newington, CT: EBTS, Volume 1, Issue 3—February, 2001

——*The Preservation of Scripture: An Answer to William Combs.* Newington, CT: EBTS, Volume 1, Issue 4—April, 2001

——*Should Fundamentalists use the NASB.* Newington, CT: EBTS, Volume 2, Issue 2—August, 2001

——*The Translation Model Predicted by Scripture.* Newington, CT: EBTS, Volume 2, Issue 3—October, 2001

——*Psalm 12:6,7 and the Permanent Preservation of God's Words.* Newington, CT: EBTS, Volume 2, Issue 5—November, 2001

——*The Lord Jesus Christ and Scribal Errors.* Newington, CT: EBTS, Volume 3, Issue 1—August-November, 2002

——*Biblical, Theological, and Religious Glossary.* Tabernacle Baptist Theological Press, 1992

——*A Critique of D.A. Carson's "The King James Version Debate."* Tabernacle Baptist Theological Press, 1992

Waite, D.A. *Bob Jones University's Inconsistent Position on the Textus Receptus and the King James Bible.* Collingswood, NJ: The Bible for Today Press, 2000

Doctrinal Terms

1. ***Bibliology:*** The study of the Bible.

2. ***Canonization:*** The process in which true believers (Old Testament and Israel; New Testament and churches) recognize which books were authoritative and binding.

3. ***Christology:*** In simple terms, this is the study of the doctrine of Christ. It is mentioned here because the modern translations weaken this doctrine.

4. ***Illumination:*** The act in which God clarifies His Word so that man can understand and apply it. It is not enough to "contend" for the faith, we must also "obey" it.

5. ***Inspiration:*** The recording, or giving of God's Word. The Holy Spirit used holy men to give us the holy Scriptures. The literal

definition of the word translated *inspiration* in 2 Timothy 3:16 is "God-breathed."

6. **Preservation:** The process in which God's Word is extended from one generation of believers to the next. This is the crux of the issue of Bible translations.

7. **Translation:** The efforts of men, hopefully but not always under God's guidance, to render God's Word into another language.

8. **Revelation:** The act whereby God communicates truth to mankind that was previously unknown (and no other way to be known). An example of revelation would be the events that took place on the days of creation. Since there was no man created yet to observe days one through five, we know about these days by God's revelation.

Textual Terms

1. **Apograph:** The preposition "apo" means "from." An apograph is a copy from the autograph.

2. **Autograph:** The original letter from the human writer. All autographs were used by the early church and are no longer in existence.

3. **Codex:** A manuscript that is in the form of a book. A codex implies that all, or a vast majority, of the books are present.

4. **Alexandrian manuscripts:** These manuscripts are dated to the fourth century. They originated in Alexandria, Egypt. They are Byzantine in the Gospels, Alexandrian in the Epistles. These manuscripts are in question by Bible-believers because of the false "Alexandrian" teachings that influenced their textual readings.

5. **Codex Sinaiticus (Aleph or A)**: A fourth century uncial manuscript of the Greek Bible, widely believed to be written between AD 330–350. Originally containing the whole of both Testaments, only portions of the Greek Old Testament or Septuagint survive along with a complete New Testament, the Epistle of Barnabas and portions of The Shepherd of Hermas. Some believe that this is one of the 50 Bibles Eusebius printed for Constantine.

6. **Codex Vaticanus (B)**: This manuscript has been housed in the Vatican Library (founded by Pope Nicholas V in 1448) for as long as it has been known, appearing in its earliest catalog of 1475 and in the 1481 catalog. Its place of origin and the history of the manuscript is uncertain, with Rome, southern Italy and Caesarea all having been suggested. There has been speculation that it had previously been in the possession of Cardinal Bessarion because the minuscule supplement has a text similar to one of Bessarion's manuscripts. T.C. Skeat, a paleographer at the British Museum, has argued that Codex Vaticanus was among the 50 Bibles that the Emperor Constantine I ordered Eusebius of Caesarea to produce. The similarity of the text with the papyri and Coptic version (including some letter formation), parallels with Athanasius' canon of AD 367 suggest an Egyptian or Alexandrian origin.

7. **Critical Text**: This "new" Greek text put forth in the late 1800s, is an attempt to reconstruct or restore the true Bible text of the New Testament by assigning a higher importance to the few "oldest manuscripts" rather than trusting the larger body of evidence in the Received Text.

   Synonyms for this text that are used throughout this book:

   • Alexandrian Text: This term implies the location of where these manuscripts are believed to have originated. In the early church, two competing "colleges" were formed. One was at Antioch, the other at Alexandria. The school of Antioch held to a literal interpretation of the words; the school at Alexandria held to an allegorical approach to interpretation and was influenced by gnosticism.

- Minority Text: This term shows that this text is based on a handful of manuscripts. The two dominant manuscripts would be Sinaiticus (Aleph) and Vaticanus (B). This "minority" is in reference to the Greek manuscripts only.

- Westcott and Hort Text: So called because the two men who paved the way for all critical text editions were Westcott and Hort, who released their text in 1881. While these men did much to lay down the theories of textual criticism, this field of study has come a great distance since their day.

- Nestle-Aland Text: This is the text often used in seminaries and Bible colleges today. This team has printed twenty-seven editions of the Critical Text.

- Eclectic Text: Webster's 1828 Dictionary defines eclectic as "Selecting; choosing; an epithet given to certain philosophers of antiquity, who did not attach themselves to any particular sect, but selected from the opinions and principles of each, what they thought solid and good. Hence we say, an eclectic philosopher; the eclectic sect." When applied to a text, the concept is that scholars supposedly took an unbiased look at all families of manuscripts and selected the best from each one.

8. *Latin Vulgate:* A translation made by Jerome in AD 382 based upon both Byzantine and Alexandrian manuscripts. It became the official translation for the Roman Catholic Church.

9. **Lectionaries**: These are not biblical manuscripts, *per se*, but were collections of Scripture lessons arranged for congregational readings. They would "contain" Scripture.

10. **Manuscripts:** Hand-written, ancient copies of scriptures from a multiplicity of cultures, languages, and eras.

11. **Minuscule**: A manuscript written in small letters. Also called "cursives."

12. **Papyrus**: An early form of paper made from the pith of the papyrus plant.

13. **Received Text:** This phrase is used to refer to the biblical manuscripts that authentic churches and Christians have accepted since the inception of the local church.

    From a biblical sense, the phrase is derived from John 17:8, where Jesus states that He has given the words to His church, and they have received them.

    This text has many synonyms that are used interchangeably throughout this book:

    • Traditional Text: This term implies that this text has been used traditionally by authentic churches.

    • Byzantine Greek Text: A synonym for the Received Text notating that it flowed throughout that Byzantine Empire, which historically correlates with early missionary efforts and apostolic writings of the first century.

    • Antiochian Text: This term is used to identify this text with the early church. It was in Antioch, Syria where believers were first called Christians. It was from this city where missionaries were first sent. It was also in this city where the Old Syriac Peshitta was translated and there is good evidence of the Old Latin Itala Bible being translated here as well. For this reason, the Antiochian Text is sometimes called the Syrian Text.

- Textus Receptus: This is the Latin phrase that is translated as "Received Text." Sometimes, the abbreviation "TR" is used to describe this text.

- Majority Text: Before 1982, the term "Majority Text" was used synonymously with Received Text, Byzantine Text, etc. Since then, two separate teams have edited a new Greek text based upon the "majority of manuscripts." This "Majority Text" agrees with the "TR" about 98–99% of the time. Yet, since there are significant differences, most people no longer use the term "Majority Text" as a synonym for the Received Text.

14. **Text:** The word *text* is used often in this book. In this context, it is a compilation of manuscript (a portion of scripture that was handwritten by early believers) evidence that is used to form the Bible. There are three competing texts for translational purposes: 1) Received Text, 2) Critical Text, and 3) Majority Text (though some classify this as synonymous with the Received Text).

15. **Uncials**: A manuscript that is written in large, capital letters. Also called a "Majuscule."

16. **Vellum**: A term for a manuscript written on expensive calfskin. This was far more superior than the ancient papyri.

17. **Version**: A term that is equivalent to "translation" but is more commonly understood to be a "redo" of a translation into a more modern format.

Important People

1. ***Theodore Beza:*** He was the successor of John Calvin at Geneva. He also continued the line of Received Text editions. His 1598 Greek edition was also used heavily by the King James translators. Beza believed his manuscripts were influenced by Waldensian Christians—an early group of Christians, outside of Catholicism, dating back to AD 120.

2. ***Dean John William Burgon:*** (1813–1888) He was an Anglican minister and "Dean of Chichester"—a staunch defender of the Traditional Text and of the "faith once delivered." He strongly opposed the methodology and theories of Westcott and Hort and the revised Greek texts.

3. ***Chrysostom:*** John Chrysostom (AD 354–407) was born in Antioch, Syria. He was born into a wealthy family but later went into a monastic life. In 386, he began preaching, earning the nickname, Chrysostom, which means "golden-mouth." After making a reference to the Empress in his sermon, he was exiled. He died during a forced march and was considered a martyr by the Syrian church.

4. ***Cyprian:*** He was bishop of Carthage and an important early Christian writer. He was probably born at the beginning of the third century in North Africa, perhaps at Carthage, where he received an excellent classical (pagan) education. After converting to Christianity, he became a bishop (AD 249) and eventually died a martyr at Carthage. Important in the area of textual debate is that he quotes from 1 John 5:7.

5. ***Erasmus:*** Erasmus was a Catholic Priest who saw and spoke out against the corruption of Catholic doctrine. He considered his life purpose to be a quest for pure scholarship. This quest caused him to reject the teachings of Rome and also prevented him from aligning closely with the Reformers. His

contribution to the textual issue is the Greek Text he edited and printed in 1516, followed by four other editions. He led the way in going back to a Greek source, rather than a Latin source for the Bible.

6. **The Fathers:** Refers to the writings of the preachers, missionaries, scholars, etc., who quoted from the Scriptures. Where their writings quote the Scriptures, they verify the Greek text as it was written in the second century onward. Anti-Nicene fathers are of particular importance since their quotes would be of a text prior to AD 325.

7. **Ignatius:** He was a pastor at Antioch, Syria, martyred in 107 by the Roman Emperor. In his writings, he consistently called Christ "the Lord Jesus Christ." In other words, he was influenced by the names of Christ as revealed in the Byzantine family rather than the shortened forms as found in the Alexandrian family.

8. **Martin Luther:** A Catholic monk who sparked the Reformation when his 95 Theses was nailed at the Wittenburg Castle on October 31, 1517.

9. **Montanus:** The group with which Tertullian identified was started by this man during the second century. Ernest William Moller, in his article, *Montanism* from Schaff-Herzog's *Encyclopedia Of Religious Knowledge*, Volume II, page 1562, speaking of Tertullian states, "To him the very substance of the Church was the Holy Spirit and by no means the Episcopacy whose right to wield the power of the keys he rejected." He further states, "Montanism was, nevertheless, not a new form of Christianity; nor were the Montanists a new sect. On the contrary, Montanism was simply a reaction of the old, the primitive church, against the obvious tendency of the day, to

strike a bargain with the world and arrange herself comfortably in it."

10. **Nestle and Aland:** Two German textual editors whose Greek texts form the basis for much of the modern New Testament translations.

11. **Origen:** Lived from AD 185–254. He followed Clement as head of the "Christian" school at Alexandria which was a blend of Gnosticism and Christianity. He was a pioneer in textual criticism and believed in an allegorical interpretation of Scripture—using symbolism rather than literal meanings of words.

12. **Polycarp:** An early Christian leader who pastored the church at Smyrna. As a disciple of John, he had first hand knowledge about apostolic writings. His letters agree with the Traditional Text.

13. **F.H.A. Scrivener:** This man lived from 1813–1891. He was a British writer and manuscript editor, and a contemporary of scholars such as Westcott and Hort. He did not share their views. After serving on the Revision Committee with Westcott and Hort, he distanced himself from that project by editing his own edition of the Received Text in 1881.

14. **Robert Stephanus:** Also known as Robert Stephens and Estienne. He continued the line of Received Text editions. His 1550 Greek edition was a major contributor to the King James translators. Incidentally, he was also the one to give us verse divisions.

15. **Tertullian:** From North Africa (probably Carthage—AD 155–225), he was a Christian apologist and writer, one of the first to write extensively in Latin. Around 195, he converted to Christianity from Paganism. Later he joined the Montanists,

a group considered heretical by the Catholic Church. He was well-educated and admired by Jerome and Cyprian. Known as the greatest theologian of the West until Augustine, he is described as brilliant, sarcastic, and intolerant. Skeptical of the value of Greek philosophy in articulating Christian truths, Tertullian asked "What has Athens to do with Jerusalem?" His treatises, thirty-one of which still exist, are arranged according to Apologetic, Disciplinary and Controversial texts. His *Apology* is dedicated to proving the social injustice directed against Christians, and his *Against Praxeas* was written to refute Modal Monarchianism. Tertullian was the first to use the term Trinitas (trinity) to describe the Godhead. In so doing, he paved the way for the development of orthodox Trinitarian and Christological doctrines.

16. ***Constantin von Tischendorf:*** A German textual critic who lived his life with the quest of restoring the true biblical text. He is credited with finding Codex Sinaiticus at St. Catherine's Greek Monastery at Mount Sinai. He believed the Textus Receptus (Received Text) did not match the original writings and set out to reconstruct the "pure text."

17. ***Dr. Samuel Tregelles:*** British scholar and editor—1813–1875. Almost entirely self-taught, Tregelles was the British Tischendorf. He did not discover as many manuscripts, and he published only one edition of his Greek text; but he too spent much of his life gathering data; he and Tischendorf frequently compared collations. At the end of his life, Tregelles prepared his single edition of the Greek text, based exclusively on the oldest manuscripts. The resultant text is generally similar to Tischendorf's, but, due to its more limited critical apparatus, does not receive much attention today. He was very influential in encouraging the work of Westcott and Hort.

18. **William Tyndale:** He was the first to translate the Bible into English from a Greek (Byzantine) source. Nearly 90% of his work is still retained in the King James Bible. He lived from 1494–1536, and died as a martyr for translating the Bible for the common man.

19. **Brooke F. Westcott and Fenton John Anthony Hort:** Dr. (Bishop) B.F. Westcott and Dr. F.J.A. Hort were both of Trinity College, Cambridge, England. These two men were leaders in the realm of Textual Criticism in the 19th Century. Their new Greek text was published in 1881, with the English Revised Version being the first translation from their work. The Americans followed suit with the American Standard Version in 1901. Their work in textual criticism laid the foundation for most future new Bible translations..

20. **John Wycliffe:** He is called the Morning Star of the Reformation. He lived from 1324–1384, and was the first to translate the Bible into Middle English using Latin manuscripts.

Translational Philosophies

1. **Allegorical Interpretation:** An interpretative process that stems from the searching of hidden meanings in the text. The literal words are not as important as the hidden or esoterical meaning to be found. This interpretative model does not emphasize the words, but rather the hidden concepts.

2. **Conflation:** An attempt to fuse together; merger of two or more things or ideas into one. In textual criticism, it is the belief of some scholars that the Byzantine Text is a merger of Alexandrian and Western texts. This allows for Byzantine readings before AD 400. This is also called the Lucian Recension or the Syrian Recension theory.

3. *Dynamic Equivalency:* A process of translating used for the NIV and many other Bible translations that attempts to interpret and convey the intent of the message and thoughts of a source text rather than the literal words.

4. *Expansions of Piety:* The belief that early copyists of Scripture added to the titles of Christ. It is asserted that the Critical Text editions did not "remove" the full names of Christ; rather, the Byzantine Text editions "added" these names as a form of piety and worship.

5. *Formal Equivalency:* also "verbal equivalency." A process of translation in which both the words and the forms of the words were rendered as closely as possible from Hebrew or Greek into English.

6. *Literal Interpretation:* An interpretative process that stems from the study of the exact words used in their context. What do these words mean? The emphasis is on the words that were deliberately chosen by the Holy Spirit.

7. *Textual Criticism:* Refers to the study of manuscripts or printings to determine the original or most authoritative form of a text. Whether one holds to a Received Text or a Critical Text, textual criticism has been employed with both of these texts. There are two types of textual criticism which determine how a textual critic approaches the Bible—one based upon belief and one based upon unbelief.

Identity of Bibles

1. *Ancient Versions:* In the textual issue, one looks not only at the Greek manuscripts, but also at what the believing churches were using in other languages.

- Old Latin (Italic): The Bible used by early Latin Christians, primarily Waldensians, a group of Christians persecuted by the organized Roman church. It is referred to as "old" because the Catholic church rejected it for the Latin Vulgate.

- Peshitta: A translation of the New Testament into the Syrian language (at Antioch) which was made in AD 150.

- Gothic: This Bible was used by Germanic tribes in central Europe during the fourth century (AD 350).

- Armenian: This Bible dates back to the fifth century and is believed to be based on the Old Syriac (Peshitta).

2. **Reformation Bibles:** During the period of the Reformation, the Bible was translated into various languages. Placing the Bible into the common man's hand had a great impact on biblical Christianity.

   - French: The Olivetan Bible (1535)

   - English: Geneva Bible (1560) by Knox, Calvin, et al

   - Spanish: The Reina Bible (1569) and the Valera (1602)

   - German: Luther Bible (1534)

   - Dutch: Statenvertaling (1618)

   - Hungarian: Vizsolyi Bible (1590)

   - Swedish: Gustav Vasa Bible, translated from Luther's Bible (1540–1541)

   This incomplete list demonstrates the effect of the Reformation of getting the Bible to every man.

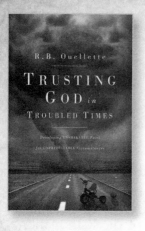
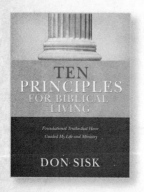
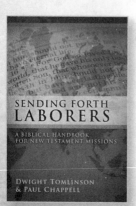